Studs Terkel

Twayne's United States Authors Series

Warren French, Editor
University College of Swansea, Wales

TUSAS 609

Studs Terkel
Photograph by Patrick Girouard

Studs Terkel

James T. Baker

Western Kentucky University

Twayne Publishers ∎ New York

Maxwell Macmillan Canada ∎ Toronto

Maxwell Macmillan International ∎ New York Oxford Singapore Sydney

Studs Terkel
James T. Baker

Twayne Publishers   Maxwell Macmillan Canada, Inc.
Macmillan Publishing Company   1200 Eglinton Avenue East
866 Third Avenue   Suite 200
New York, New York 10022   Don Mills, Ontario M3C 3N1

Macmillan Publishing Company is part of the Maxwell Communications Group of Companies.

Library of Congress Cataloging-in-Publication Data

Baker, James Thomas.
    Studs Terkel / James T. Baker.
    p. cm. – (Twayne's United States authors series; TUSAS 609)
    Includes bibliographical references and index.
    ISBN 0-8057-7638-9 (alk. paper)
    1. Terkel, Studs, 1912- – Literary art. I. Title. II. Series.
PN1990.72.T4B34 1992
973.9'092 – dc20   92-3856
[B]   CIP

10 9 8 7 6 5 4 3 2 1

Printed in the United States of America.

For

Marvin and Mildred Baker

The First Family of Texas

Contents

Preface

The February day I drove Studs Terkel from a morning breakfast conversation with students at Alabama's Auburn University to the Atlanta airport was a warm one. He had been up late the night before having dinner with his old friend Virginia Durr, was up at 6:00 A.M. for the breakfast, and at noon was fresh and energetic. He waved off my offer of lunch and told me that he preferred just to talk.

He spoke constantly of the people he had interviewed over the past 25 years. He recalled their names, how he had met them, the circumstances under which he had recorded their words, even the way they spoke. I had only to mention a name, and he was off on a verbatim recitation of a passage from one or another of his oral histories.

He spoke of the 1988 presidential election, which greatly disturbed him, and of his dismay that the Democrats preferred losing with someone safe than winning with a reformer. He thought it was pathetic the way George Bush had twisted the word *liberal* into something negative. "I could've answered Bush on that one," he huffed. "I would've said, 'Look up the word. It means, first, generous. Do you think that's bad? Second, it means being tolerant of others. Is that bad?' I could've shut him up." He chuckled.

"What we need in America is a little *glasnost* of our own," he continued. "Open up. Admit we were wrong in Vietnam. Admit our system hasn't helped the poor among us." He considered it for a moment. "You know what Grenada was? America was John Wayne, walking down the street with a bloody nose from Vietnam. The boys on the block were laughing. He saw little Grenada, Woody Allen, and he decided he'd regain some pride by beating the hell out of him. It made him feel pretty good too. So he may do it again. Just helps to smack someone." Panama and Iraq were in the future but not unforeseen by Studs Terkel.

At the airport we rode an underground train to the American

Airlines terminal. The disembodied voice on the train, giving us orders, sounded like "Hal" in Stanley Kubrick's 1968 film *2001: A Space Odyssey*, and it made Terkel speculate: "It would have been easier to put a human voice in here – so why the android? Why a machine to tell humans what to do?" He gave it some thought, careful to obey Hal's orders. "I've got it!" he said gleefully. "It's because people will do what a machine says before what a man says. The man's gotta sound like a machine."

As we were parting I finally made my suggestion. After his next book, the one on race, I hoped he would write one on America's internal migrants. He perked up. I explained: Appalachian whites in Detroit; Alabama blacks in Chicago; Corn Huskers in California; New York Jews in Miami. How it feels, reestablishing yourself in a new land, when that land is still America.

"I know what I'd call it," Terkel said. "Nomads."

We shook hands, and he said, "Take it easy – but take it." He grinned before he left: "That's an old labor slogan. I have no idea what it means."

■

Studs Terkel is a caricaturist's delight. Benjamin DeMott has described him as "short, tousled, raffish, impish," with a "near wordless garrulity."[1] Herbert Mitgang called him "a scholar disguised as a leprecaun."[2] Norman Mark found him just millimeters from ugly – his nose searching for a right hook, his chin wandering about with a mind of its own, his voice like gravel hitting hot tar – yet completely charming.[3] Tom Fitzpatrick said he looked like a man born just a bit too late to be a vaudeville stand-up comic.[4] Joanne Koch said that when dressed in a tuxedo he looked "like a bookie going to his sister's wedding."[5] Terkel himself, not one for false modesty, once allowed that at best he looked like "a minor mob figure the day after he died."[6]

Yet despite having the face, voice, and costume of a comedian, Terkel has produced more serious literature than many "serious" writers. A Chicagoan of Jewish ancestry and comfortable means, he has, in searching for the truth about his country, become a spokesman for the common American of all regions and religions. An entertainer, radio-show host, disc jockey, he has established himself as one of the world's best-known oral historians.

Interesting contradictions abound in his life. He is an expert on American ethnic minorities, many of them far removed from his own urbanity. A white Jewish man, he is often at home in a black Baptist church listening to the gospel music of Mahalia Jackson. Reared in a thoroughly capitalist home by a mother who dreamed of riches, he is a socialist. Fervently devoted to Chicago, "The City That Works," he rejects its political values and considers the agrarian Progressive Robert La Follette his hero.

Although Terkel has made a successful career out of asking people questions about themselves, he assiduously avoids being questioned about his own life. He readily consents to interviews on politics (declining to say whether he was ever a Communist), current events, and music. He has published a book of personal memoirs and flavored other books with scenes from his life. Yet he grows nervous and uncommunicative when anyone tries to ask him (as Paul Newman and Joan Crawford have without success) about certain parts of his colorful life. In *Talking to Myself: A Memoir of My Times* (1977) he admits that he has concealed a great deal of himself because "there is a private domain on which I'll not trespass."[7]

Still more interesting is his apparent disorganization. For a person who has written and performed in media that demand split-second timing, who has produced solidly well-structured books and television programs, Terkel is a wildly misarranged individual. If in a speech he wants to make four points, he will back into the third, circle without actually touching the second, stumble over the fourth, and slide past the first. He is still one of the most entertaining and effective of modern public speakers, and he has lived one of the most fulfilling of "disorganized" lives.

A small, fragile boy who grew up to be a whiskey-drinking, cigar-smoking workaholic, Terkel is healthy and going full speed, his fame at its zenith, in his eighty-first year. When he was 76 he produced still another of his oral histories, *The Great Divide: Second Thoughts on the American Dream* (1988); appeared in the feature film *Eight Men Out;* and was the subject of a lead *TV Guide* article on the way the media cover politics.

Everything about Terkel – his appearance, his accomplishments, his life-style – is part of a fascinating pattern that follows its own peculiar logic. He was right to dictate his memoirs into a tape recorder, in stream-of-consciousness fashion, because that may be

the only way to capture his mind and life. Still, most of us long for
more linear movement, logical consistency, cause and effect – things
I hope to provide in this book, the first critical study of Terkel's life
and work only because he is not yet considered beyond his prime
and ready for serious study. I count myself fortunate to be the first. I
know I shall not be the last.

Chronology

Chapter One

From Chicago's Child
to "Red" Actor

The man who became Studs Terkel was born in the Bronx, New York, on 16 May 1912, within a year of three American presidents: Gerald Ford and Ronald Reagan (both 1911) and Richard Nixon (1913). Typically, he has never acknowledged generational ties with any of them, preferring in his lighthearted manner to identify his birth with the death of the ill-fated *Titanic*. "Me and *Titanic* – it went down and I came up," he jokes.

His parents, Samuel and Anna Finkel Terkel, both Jewish, had just 10 years earlier come to America from the "old country, somewhere around the Polish-Russian border," Terkel has said.[1] Sam Terkel was by trade a tailor, his wife a seamstress. Sam was frail and retiring and a lover of music; Anna was robust and "feverish" and a lover of money. Terkel was the third and last of three sons. A brother Meyer was six, a brother Ben five, when "the baby" was born.

Sam and Anna named their baby Louis. Later, after he had become famous as "Studs," he wrote that as a boy he was called "Loo-iss," as in Lewis Stone, the prisoner of Zenda, not "Loo-ee," as in Louis the Sun King of France (*Talking*, 11). He was Louis Terkel throughout his public school and university years, as well as through the early 1930s as he worked at various New Deal jobs. It was in show business that he became Studs, and only in time was Louis dropped completely. He was Louis Terkel on the title pages of his first few books, then Louis "Studs" Terkel, and finally Studs Terkel. From the first the name Terkel was a bit of a joke, "not what you think and I wish," he says in public appearances.

In August 1921, when Terkel was nine, his life took a dramatic turn – for the better it now seems. With his father's health on the decline, with the future uncertain, his mother found a rooming

1

house in Chicago to manage, and the Terkels headed toward what they considered the American frontier, "the wild West." Chicago then became Terkel's town, the city on earth he loved best, the center of his life for the rest of the century, the subject of his books.

His playmates in the Bronx, seeing him off on the train, warned him to beware of the Indians out there. They had heard that the Chicago Black Hawks were a dangerous tribe. Terkel still vividly recalls his trip to "Indian territory," feeling like the English butler Ruggles on his way to Red Gap, expecting at any moment to see painted faces and war bonnets. He says he sat up all night watching for trouble, refusing to close his eyes for fear he would miss the excitement of a raid.[2] Instead of Indian villages, of course, he saw small, sleepy towns whose names he can still remember (*Dreams*, xvii). Nor has he forgotten that his one meal on the train was a cheese sandwich and carton of milk his mother bought from a vendor in Buffalo. Already his fertile imagination was mixing with a sharp memory for people and places.

He remembers arriving at Chicago's LaSalle Street train station, taking his first breath of stockyards air, being met by his brothers, who had gone before him, observing for the first time the peculiar combinations of Chicago humanity (*Dreams*, xviii). There were wealthy people with acres of leather baggage; recently arrived immigrants toting cardboard boxes and speaking broken English; scores of eager black porters, all apparently named George. On the platform his brother Ben turned his cap around for him, as if to say he was entering a new life, and he felt his head spin with excitement. Things were happening here in this young raw city, and those things were about to happen to him (*Chicago*, 33). The arrival in Chicago was Terkel's discovery of America.

He would grow up, be educated, and find his measure of fame in this city of Jane Addams and Al Capone. Here the character "Studs" would be born, a character known all over the nation and in other countries. In time he would be one of the most universally recognized voices of Chicago, and to his listeners and readers Chicago would be the city of Studs Terkel.

In the Bronx Terkel had suffered from chronic asthma, and for a time after he moved to Chicago the attacks persisted. During the summers of 1923 and 1924 he was sent to the Mount Pleasant lakeside resort in Michigan, a place where ailing and moderately affluent people of all ages shared long, slow days of sunshine, quiet meals, and afternoon radio shows. It was there, as he listened intently to baseball games, President Warren G. Harding's funeral service, and the chaos of the 1924 Democratic National Convention, that he began his love affair with the wireless. At puberty his health improved, and he went on to pursue a strenuous career, much of it in radio. The Windy City proved good for him, as did radio.

Family

Terkel was educated in Chicago public schools and at the University of Chicago. He learned perhaps more at home than he did at school. His most important education no doubt came on the streets of the city.

Sam Terkel's health, unlike that of his son, did not improve; still, he always had or made time for Terkel. He took him to musical concerts and shared radio programs with him. On their crystal set they followed live reports from Kentucky on the plight of trapped cave explorer Floyd Collins and from Tennessee on the Dayton "monkey" trial of John T. Scopes, which was argued by Clarence Darrow and William Jennings Bryan (*Chicago*, 120). Terkel still remembers his father as a "marvelous" and lovable man. Sam died in 1931, when Terkel was a 19-year-old university student.[3]

His mother, Anna, was a different story. Terkel has always compared her with the mother of Thomas Wolfe in Wolfe's 1929 novel *Look Homeward, Angel* (Katz, 3). In Chicago, in her role as innkeeper, she became a bona fide American capitalist. As manager of the two establishments that she and Sam kept, she developed a keen eye for profit. The first, which they had from 1921 to 1925, was a rooming house at the corner of Ashland and Flournoy, on the near west side, adjacent to Cook County Hospital, at that time the world's largest medical center. Most of the Terkels' guests were connected with one or another of the hospital's services. The whole family worked there. Terkel changed sheets, worked the night desk, and treated beds for parasites. His brother Ben, the "skirt chaser" of the family, comforted lonely nurses (*Chicago*, 45).

In 1925 the family moved up the economic ladder to manage a larger establishment, a residential hotel called the Wells-Grand after the two streets that met outside. It had 50 rooms and efficiency flats and was owned by Henry L. Flentye, a man Terkel describes as a conservative "McKinley Republican." Flentye liked doing business with Sam Terkel, whom he trusted, and he tolerated Anna, who for four years made the place pay handsome dividends both to Flentye and to the Terkels. Late in 1929, however, things went wrong: for Anna, for Flentye, and for the nation. Anna withdrew the considerable family savings from the Reliance State Bank just before it closed. But she invested it all in magnate Samuel Insull's utilities company, and when Insull went bankrupt in a nationally noted collapse, she lost everything. As Terkel puts it, when the tycoons she so admired and trusted goofed, "Kerplunk went her American Dream" (*Dreams*, xxiii). Although she held on to the Wells-Grand and kept her family fed, for the rest of her life she felt like a failure. According to Terkel, she died "a bitter, cantankerous old woman, who almost, though never quite, caught the brass ring" (*Dreams*, xxiv).

The Great Depression (*Hard Times* Terkel would name it) hit the Wells-Grand as hard as it did the Terkel family's nest egg. The pool of skilled laborers that fed its steady stream of patrons began drying up. For Terkel the symbol of the depression is still the big VACANCY sign in the hotel window.[4] Flentye argued for a long time that the downturn was part of a normal economic cycle and simply adjusted his rates to accommodate a less affluent clientele. He was not prepared to go as far in that direction as Anna was, and the two of them came to verbal blows over her policies. After Sam died in 1931 there was no one to mediate between them, and they battled ever more fiercely over her liberal attitude toward questionable tenancy (*Chicago*, 77). As Terkel puts it, delicately, there was always room at Anna's inn, particularly for young couples without luggage interested in brief encounters. In his mother's Bible they found "the winking Gospels" (*Hard Times*, 5).

Finally in 1937, after years of struggle, Anna lost her hotel. She never lost her influence on Terkel, however, even though it is obvious from his writings and the direction his life took that he admired and identified more with his father than with his mother. His dreams and values are not hers. Yet in ways he does not admit, perhaps does not recognize, he inherited much from her: vitality, intelligence, and an aggressive pursuit of goals, even if his goals are not hers.

Terkel was influenced by his brothers as well, although apparently in lesser measure and for a briefer time. Mayer, the eldest, the "intellectual" of the family, taught Terkel to read and write and perhaps to reason. The middle son, Ben, "the randy one," as Terkel calls him, was his pal. Ben worked more or less steadily as a shoe salesman at The Boston Store, at the corner of State and Madison, "the busiest corner in the world," but in his spare time he practiced the art of love. Not only did he comfort nurses; he picked up girls at Chicago nightspots and brought them to vacant rooms at the Wells-Grand. Terkel says that he often played Leporello to Ben's Don Juan. Working the night desk, he let Ben and his lady of the evening into a room, kept watch for them, and later changed the sheets so that his mother would not know what had happened. As a reward Ben took Terkel to hear jazz played at the Dreamland Ballroom and kept him supplied with the sheet music of current pop hits (*Chicago*, 45).

Once Terkel actually saved Ben's life when Ben foolishly picked up the girlfriend of a local mobster and was caught with her. Terkel rushed up to the scene of an accident about to happen, concocted a story about a sick mother who needed Ben at home, and persuaded the tough guy to let his brother off with a warning. He was amazed when, years later, he saw Vittorio De Sica's 1948 film *The Bicycle Thief* and noted how much its final scene was like his own real-life experience that night with Ben (*Talking*, 17-20). This would not be Terkel's only brush with the mob; nor was it always Ben who was in danger. Ben later saved Terkel's life to even the score.

Hotel

Perhaps as great an influence on Terkel as his family was his boyhood home, the Wells-Grand. He literally grew up in its lobby. His family moved there when he was 13, and his mother kept it until he was 25 and on his own. It was inhabited mostly by single men, with a few flats reserved for married couples. In good times, before the depression, its tenants were solvent, approaching modest affluence; in bad times, after 1929, they more often than not were barely able to pay their rent. Both in good times and in bad they were a volatile mixture of liberals and conservatives, union men and managers, and over games of cribbage and hearts they carried on spirited debates about government and the economy (*Chicago*, 76). There were followers of Eugene V. Debs and disciples of Father Charles Coughlin, and Terkel relished their arguments, even when on occasion they turned violent. Of all the schools he attended, he says, the Lobby School was the best.[5]

One of the guests of that era introduced Terkel to a series of miniature paperbound volumes called the E. Haldeman-Julius Blue Books, each one of which featured a collection of the essential writings of a famous philosopher. They came 20 for $1 from a mail-order company in Girard, Kansas. Terkel devoured and digested the whole series, matching wits with such seminal thinkers as Rousseau, Voltaire, Jefferson, Thomas Paine, and Gandhi. He in fact recalls the time he was reading Gandhi, all full of the sacredness of life, and refused his mother's order to apply a blowtorch to hotel bedsprings to kill bugs (*Talking*, 112).

At Christmas 1977 the *Chicago Tribune* asked several prominent Chicagoans, Terkel among them, to recall their most memorable Christmas. Terkel unhesitatingly chose the Christmas of 1928, the year he was 16, at the time he was discovering philosophy. The Wells-Grand guests were playing cards in the lobby, killing a pint of whiskey, telling tall tales, and singing Pennsylvania Dutch folk songs. Through the snowy air, during a pause in the festivities, Terkel heard the *Tribune* tower chimes playing "Hark, the Herald Angels Sing" and thought what a perfect way this was to celebrate the birthday of the Prince of Peace.[6] The Christmas of 1933, another Christmas spent in that lobby, was, on the other hand, the worst of holidays. Terkel's father had died, and hard times had come to Chicago (*Talking*, 33-36).

Still, even bad times at the hotel were formative and educational. Terkel recalls with a sense of shame the time he opened the door of a flat so that the police could arrest a guest. Even though the man was guilty of bank robbery, Terkel felt like a traitor for helping entrap him, and he felt even worse when the police called him "a good citizen." He was called good for being bad, for betraying a man who had not harmed him, who had trusted him, a man who showed no anger when he saw what Terkel had done (*Talking*, 93-103).

Music

From his early youth Terkel was moved by music. He responded instinctively to its sounds and rhythms, spent a great deal of time during his school days pursuing its charms, and as an adult formed long-lasting and comfortable friendships with its composers and performers. He has made a career out of introducing it to audiences on stage and radio. Although he could never sing or play an instrument, he has done more than most people to promote musicians and their music – in all its fascinating variety.

Chicago was, of course, the perfect city in which to experience that variety. It offered him frontier music from the Great Plains, ethnic European folk music from the tight neighborhoods of recent immigrants, mountain music brought to town by refugees from impoverished Appalachia, and perhaps most significantly the jazz and gospel songs of blacks fleeing Dixie.

Terkel has always demonstrated a particular fondness for the black music he encountered as a young man. He spent many teenage nights outside Chicago nightspots listening to the improvisations of black bands (*Dreams*, 8). During his dreary years in law school he took comfort in live black performances on the South Side as well as from nickel-apiece "race records" just beginning to find their way to sidewalk music stands. When he broke into radio he introduced first to Chicago and later to the nation all the colors of his musical rainbow, especially the black one.

His first book, *Giants of Jazz* (1957), which he wrote in the late 1940s and early 1950s, demonstrates his affection for and wide knowledge of a type of black music previously ignored by white scholars and most white audiences. He counted among his closest friends two black musicians, bluesman Big Bill Broonzy and gospel singer Mahalia Jackson. He still wonders why music has failed to make America a fully integrated society. While whites have come to appreciate black music, jazz, blues, gospel, all owing at least partly to Terkel's shows, the races are as far apart socially as ever, perhaps more so. He loves to recall the night in June 1938 that Joe Louis defeated Max Schmeling, when he and a pal named Dude wandered into the black south Chicago ghetto, celebrated with blacks, and shared their food and booze (*Chicago*, 106-8). Such experiences are now rare for white men.

Terkel is not like most white men. In black music he learned to hear cries of anguish and expressions of hope. He turned his sensitive ear to other music, and in all the variety he heard such cries and expressions, each group expressing them in its own unique way. He began meeting composers and performers, interviewing them for his radio shows, educating himself and his audiences in the subtleties of sound. He became a musicologist, then a biographer, then a folklorist, and finally an oral historian.

Politics

Terkel grew up in Chicago's famous (some say infamous) Forty-second Ward, a place remembered 50 years later as a hotbed of radical politics.[7] As early as 1923, when he was 11 and the Harding scandals began to break, he listened intently as union men argued that the whole of government was corrupt and needed shaking up and as their conservative sparring partners advised them to move to Russia, where they would find the kind of society they obviously preferred.

He attended his first political rally that year, walking with Ben the two blocks from his home to the old Ashland Auditorium, where he listened to an evening of entertainment and speeches in support of the Democratic candidate for mayor, Judge William E. Dever. There were acrobats, wrestlers, exotic dancers, and a string of golden-tongued, spread-eagle orators (*Chicago*, 21-24). When Dever won the election Terkel wondered about a system in which a bizarre spectacle like that would bring political success.

The following year, 1924, he returned to the Ashland to hear Burton K. Wheeler, who was Robert La Follette's vice-presidential running mate on the Progressive party ticket. Wheeler apparently made good sense to the 12-year-old Terkel that night, because he was persuaded to give his heart to La Follette-Wheeler and progressivism. At public school that fall Miss Henrietta Boone, who expected all of her young gentlemen to be for President Coolidge, was shocked when Terkel announced he was for "Fightin' Bob La Follette." He had a chance to interview Wheeler some 45 years later, and while by that time they disagreed on many matters, Terkel still credited him with helping form his own Progressive political philosophy.

His low opinion and rejection of politics-as-usual, Chicago style, grew stronger during the 1930s when twice he served as a poll watcher. The first time, in November 1930, he made $5 watching for Independent candidate for the state senate Mary Daley, who was running for her recently deceased husband's seat. He learned that day that Red Kelly, the man who had recruited him for Daley, was hedging his bets by working for the candidates of all three parties, Democratic, Republican, and Independent. There was little difference between the candidates, and their supporters were less than devout (*Talking*, 71-83).

In May 1934 Terkel was sent to watch at a skid-row precinct and observed blatant fraud and bribery. A court trial later in the year charged a few local captains with voting irregularities, but because Terkel was convinced that the real crooks were in city hall giving these small fry their orders, he "forgot" what he had seen. Just as earlier he had been called a good citizen for entrapping a hotel guest, now he was called a bad citizen for not helping convict the captains. Bad was good, good was bad. A fellow watcher did remember what he saw, testified to it, and had his leg broken as a reward. For a time Terkel was himself in danger, but his brother Ben called on one Prince Arthur Quinn to get him off the hook (*Talking*, 84-92). The earlier debt, when Terkel saved Ben, was thus repaid.

Such episodes and experiences only confirmed Terkel's conviction that American politics as practiced in Chicago, "Irish" style, was hopeless.

School

While Terkel got much of his education at home and on Chicago streets, he did go to regular school. The classroom may not have been the most formative of his several educations, but it seems to have been academically effective. He has often spoken disparagingly of reactionary teachers, criminally inclined classmates, and boring subject matter, yet he exhibits all the marks of a man well served by formal education. He loves to read, and he writes well. He appreciates and understands philosophy and history. He continues to search and think and learn, firmly wedded to the lifelong quest for wisdom, an educated man.

The Chicago public schools he attended were neither exclusive
nor academically distinguished. From 1921 to 1925 he attended the
McLarren School at the corner of Flournoy and Laflin, a rough
school with tough students, many of them the sons of recent immigrants, with names like Marco, Orlando, Baccala, Jimmy One, and
Jimmy Two. Jimmy One went into the jukebox business and grew
rich and respectable; Jimmy Two went into the protection racket and
was found shot dead in an alley (*Chicago*, 13, 54). From these boys
Terkel learned his first lessons in human nature. In the 1980s McLarren was razed to make way for a housing project (*Chicago*, 56).

Between 1925 and 1928, the best of times for the Terkel family,
Terkel attended McKinley High School, Chicago's oldest public high
school, which counted among its graduates the famous cinematogra-
pher Walt Disney. His teachers there, as he remembers them, were
scholarly "Presbyterian" types: Francis Brimblecome, Olive Leekley,
Elmer Potter, George Commons – names and personalities out of a
Dickens novel. There his classmates continued to be the rough-and-
tumble sons of immigrants, all looking for a leg up the economic ladder. For many of them, including one Louis Fratto, the way up was
organized crime. At a McKinley High alumni luncheon in the 1950s,
when Fratto was daily appearing before the televised Kefauver Senate Crime Committee hearings, Terkel "went over like a lead bal-
loon" when in a brief speech he facetiously boasted that while other
schools had produced boring lawyers and bankers, McKinley had
produced television stars (*Talking*, 16).

At McKinley Terkel was a debater. He was given a strong push in
that direction by his old pal Jimmy Two, who told him that he
needed to practice his persuasive skills so that when he became a
lawyer he could defend his classmates in court. Jimmy Two was
already making money on the down side of the law. When the debate
topic was capital punishment, Terkel asked to argue the negative.
But his coach made him take the affirmative, and Terkel led his team
to victory arguing for something he did not believe. After the debate
Jimmy Two slipped him $5, saying, "All traitors should be strung up
by da nuts" (*Talking*, 234). It was a strange point to be made by a
boy who might well one day be facing the death penalty. It convinced Terkel that while he might have a gift for debate, perhaps for
the law, and while his gift might be profitable, it was all sophistry.

Terkel has always held mixed feelings about the mob. Some of his classmates ended up in it. For all its evils, he seemed once to be saying, it offered a way out of poverty for some otherwise pretty hopeless guys (DeMott, 84). It was, in fact, not a great deal worse to him than Chicago politics. As for McKinley High, it became an all-black school – in Terkel's words, "Willie and Booker replaced Vito and Maurice" – and went from winning debates to winning state championships in basketball. It too was eventually razed for urban renewal (*Chicago*, 55).

In 1928, at age 16, Terkel entered the University of Chicago. In 1932, at 20, after his mother had lost the family savings and his father had died, he received his Ph.B. With the country in the grips of a depression and himself without clear career goals, Terkel went on to study at the university's School of Law. He received his J.D. on schedule in 1934, but it took two tries for him to pass the Illinois bar (Terry, 8).

He never practiced law. He never defended his old classmates. Even today he is vague about why he sloshed through a program, preparing for a profession, when he hated every minute of it and had no intention of practicing it. He did admire the famous Chicago trial lawyer Clarence Darrow, who had defended the Jewish boys Leopold and Loeb and the Tennessee teacher John T. Scopes, but whether that admiration made him want to study law is uncertain. In 1976, when he was one of several Chicagoans asked by the *Tribune* to name childhood heroes, Terkel chose Darrow. "He was his own man," he said. "It was as simple as that."[8] In 1963 Terkel had, appropriately enough, won the Clarence Darrow Commemorative Award for service to his fellow man, although he won it not for practicing law but for reporting.

Whatever his motives for studying law, Terkel never liked law school and seems early to have decided that he would not make it his life's work. While he has rarely commented on his undergraduate years, he has many times spoken, always negatively, about his two years at Chicago Law. He was bored; he felt he was wasting time; he could not make himself study or pay attention.[9] He can now recall only one case his class studied, one involving statutory rape, during the 24 months he struggled to stay awake.

Near the end of this struggle, looking for a way to avoid some corporation's law office, Terkel applied for a job with the Federal

Bureau of Investigation. He was interviewed by the man who "got" John Dillinger. When the man asked him why a Chicago graduate would want a $1,260-a-year job classifying fingerprints, Terkel could not come up with a convincing answer, and he was never called back for further discussion (*Talking*, 126).

Terkel failed his bar examination the first time around, when 90 percent of his high-powered classmates passed. He did scrape through the second time, but he never appeared in court as an attorney. From day one he was out of step with his fellow students, and after graduation he continued to march to his own jazz drummer. A vote taken at a 1960 reunion of the Chicago Law class of 1934 on its members' preference in that year's presidential election found 45 for Nixon, 41 for Kennedy, and 1 for "Fightin' Bob La Follette." The other 86 members laughed indulgently, knowing that it was "good old Studs" who had cast the dissenting vote (*Talking*, 11). Yet in the long run Terkel has become the class's most famous member. In 1969 the University of Chicago Alumni Association named him its Communicator of the Year.

Hard Times and a "Good" War

America was five years into the Great Depression and two years into the New Deal when Terkel finally passed the bar. At age 22 he had little idea what to do with his life, as in certain ways he has continued throughout his adult life not to know. "I just 'ad hoc' it – improvise," he explains (Fiffer, 55). This was and is not a bad dilemma for a creative person. It makes for an openness to opportunity and willingness to take chances.

Terkel worked for a time with sociologist Philip Hauser, doing opinion polls and surveys among the unemployed, good field training for the radio interviews and oral histories he would one day do (Koch, 84). Later on, in Washington, he counted baby bonds and did odd jobs for the Federal Emergency Rehabilitation Administration (*Talking*, 89). For a time, after returning to Chicago, he ran a movie theater. Then in 1938 he joined the Illinois branch of the Works Project Administration (WPA) Writers Project, Radio Division. At long last, in this program, he found work he truly enjoyed.

One of his first assignments was to write scripts inspired by masterpieces at the Chicago Art Institute (*Hard Times*, 9). They were aired on Chicago radio station WGN, the voice of the *Chicago Tribune*, more specifically the voice of its owner, Colonel Robert R. McCormick, a man known for his condemnation of intellectuals and their schemes for social reform. This was Terkel's debut in radio, as a writer, and it was in this medium that he began his climb to fame.

The days with the Writers Project earned Terkel several lifelong friends, among them black novelist Richard Wright and white novelist Nelson Algren. Algren became his closest literary confidant. Terkel loved Algren both as a person and as a writer, and he identified with his characters, particularly with the wonderful Some Fellow Willie. He was incensed by what he considered the shameful way academia and "that Eastern bunch" of snobbish critics ignored Algren, whom he considered the best of modern writers – and the funniest man he ever knew. Algren's humor, he believed, belay a deeply serious mind, one that had to laugh in order to keep its balance. Algren's horses, Terkel wrote when Algren died in 1981, usually ran out of the money. His luck was not good; he was never praised by powerful literary brokers or endowed by great universities; yet he kept shuffling along, as do all true winners, to immortality.[10]

Although he was declared a "nonperson" by the literary establishment, Algren left an impressive group of books, a number of which profoundly influenced Terkel. *Chicago: City on the Make* (1951), for example, provided both inspiration and model for Terkel's *Division Street: America* (1967) and *Chicago* (1986), and Terkel readily acknowledged his debt: "My own writing – for better or worse – was influenced by Nelson more than anybody I know" (Terry, 9).

It was also in the 1930s, as he moved from job to job, that Terkel became an actor. The old high school debater with a flair for the dramatic gesture fell in love with the stage. As early as 1934, the year he left Chicago Law, he began playing in operas. As a Sevillean in *Carmen* he fought a loose stocking that kept falling down during the performance, much to the delight of the audience. He made it without memorable incident through *Turandot* as a lowly member of the crowd. And in *Lohengrin* he was a somewhat diminutive Teutonic knight who found it hard to bear his heavy chain-mail costume

(*Talking,* 254-56). Modest as these peripheral efforts were, they whetted his appetite for acting and set him on his thespian journey.

In 1937 he joined the Chicago Repertory Theater, which was then known as daring, experimental, and socially active. On and off stage its members fought for liberal causes, and Terkel joined right in, by night treading hardwood and by day pounding concrete, fighting for rent control and against the poll tax. Though this left-wing activism returned to haunt him, he never regretted those days when he was considered a bad citizen for doing so many things right (*Talking,* 84-103).

He relished being Citizen Terkel in those days. On his way to rehearsal one evening in 1935, he was picked up and detained by the notorious, strikebreaking Chicago "Red Squad," at that time one of the city's most feared vigilante groups. He was in a phase of his life when he relished affecting a "gangster" appearance. The squad leader asked him who he was, and Terkel replied flippantly that as a matter of fact he was a citizen. The presumptuous answer almost earned him a beating. Only his invincible gift for gab let him escape intact, with only a few dire threats against his future well-being (*Talking,* 119).

In his first role for Chicago Rep, also in 1935, Terkel played the cabbie Joe in Clifford Odets's *Waiting for Lefty.* First produced in New York just two years earlier, *Lefty* was still fresh to the American theater and was just the kind of political-statement drama the Chicago group loved to do. Furthermore, at that time Chicago was in the midst of the same sort of cab drivers' strike featured in the play. *Lefty* was short, was simply told, required minimal sets, and could be produced just about anywhere, if not to just any audience. It had easily identifiable good guys and bad guys, and it blamed the ills that beset the working class on bourgeois managers and the corrupt labor leaders they could so easily bribe to do their bidding.

As the play opens a desperate but frightened band of drivers wait for their charismatic leader, Lefty Costello, to return with a plan of action. They fear being labeled Reds by a society that is slowly starving them. Lefty is found murdered, presumably because he cannot be bought, and the drivers are transformed. They discuss the philosophy of Karl Marx, plot a revolt, and go off shouting, "Strike! Strike! Strike!"

It is a powerful play, despite its simplistic plot and philosophy, and Terkel's cast apparently played it well, once almost too well. At a performance arranged for a group of striking cabbies, the actor identified in the course of the action as traitor to the movement was attacked by the audience and came close to being beaten. Terkel and the other members of the cast had to stop the play and explain to the cabbies that this poor guy was just playing his part as it was written. At last they settled down and watched the story to its end.

It is ironic that in his very first stage role – and in so many roles since that time – Terkel played a driver, for in real life he has never learned to drive a car. In Chicago he has always taken cabs or buses, and when away from home he has, in his words, always depended – like Blanche DuBois – on the kindness of strangers (Katz, 3). When on an early television show he drove a car in a gasoline commercial, he was in fact merely turning the wheel. A crew of men off-camera pushed the vehicle; the engine was kept safely disconnected (Koch, 84-86). In the late 1980s, when Terkel played a cabbie in the film adaptation of the Harriette Arnow novel *The Dollmaker*, the director used a stand-in when the cab was in motion.

It was while playing in Chicago Rep that Terkel got his nickname. On the fiction best-seller list for 1935 was the trilogy *Studs Lonigan* by James T. Farrell. The story was set in Chicago, and Terkel fell in love with it. He carried copies around with him everywhere he went. His friends and fellow actors, noticing his addiction, began calling him Studs, and the name, as is the case with names that are particularly appropriate or inappropriate, stuck (Fitzpatrick, 8). In this case it seems to have been the name's inappropriateness that did the trick. No one could have been less like Farrell's Studs – ghetto Irish, anti-Semitic, criminally inclined – than the new Studs Terkel.

Terkel's wife, Ida, never liked the name. To her it smacked of the gangster image he was cultivating when they met in 1938. Her low opinion of it, her suspicion that it could easily be misunderstood and misinterpreted, has been confirmed many times. Perhaps the most hilarious example of her discomfort with it occurred when Nelson Algren had the Terkels paged in the Paris airport. The French announcer's voice echoed through the terminal: "Mrs. Ida Terkel – and stud" (Koch, 87).

Writing for the radio and acting on the stage, complementary endeavors as it turned out, led Terkel to a third field, a synthesis of the first two, radio acting. He became a voice, a quite distinct voice, for the network soap operas being written and produced in Chicago in those days.

Early radio flourished in Chicago before it shifted to the two coasts, and the accent of the early Chicago announcers, mostly men from the plains west of the city, became standard American Radio English. To this day their "accentless" pronunciation is taught to aspiring young radio and television announcers, in much the same way the Oxbridge pronunciation, known as standard BBC English, is taught to aspiring young British announcers.

That Terkel could never manage the standard pronunciation made him both a marketable talent and an actor with limited range. He spoke with a Bronx-Loop twang, that sound of "gravel hitting hot tar," an accent that radio directors called gangster English. His appearance, when he read for parts, only sharpened the stereotype. As early as 1933, when he was still in law school, his face was "crooked" enough to land him on the cover of *Official Detective* magazine, wearing a pearl gray fedora that cost him half the $10 he earned for posing. After the photo session the hat blew away in a Chicago breeze and disappeared forever down Michigan Avenue, but the cover photo brought him a measure of fame (Koch, 87). One of Al Capone's pimps, Dennis Cooney, let it be known that Terkel could come work for him at "Da Winch" (the Winchmore Hotel, a Capone brothel) anytime he wished (*Talking*, 30-31). Terkel passed up the offer.

Still, he went to interviews, knowing that, with his coat collar turned up and his hat brim down over his forehead, he looked like a gangster. And he got a lot of parts, all of them involving characters on the wrong side of the law. He was first the big-city mobster Butch Malone in the series "Ma Perkins." For six weeks he pestered, threatened, and terrorized the good citizens of Ma's pristine small American town, until he was nabbed by the cops and sent along to Sing Sing (*Talking*, 150).

Soon he resurfaced as another gangster, with a different name but the same voice, message, and mission, the "Chicago Kid" type of mobster, on another show. Show followed show. He was Butch or Bugs, Pete or Bullets, in "The Romance of Helen Trent," "Girls Alone," "Secret City," and "First Nighter." He specialized in the intimidation of such all-American female stars as Mary Martin, Kitty

Keane, and Mercedes McCambridge (Koch, 84). On election night 1980, while watching a news program about victor Ronald Reagan, Terkel learned that Reagan's mother-in-law, Edie Davis, had once played opposite him on the show "Betty and Bob" as Betty's mother. (Terkel, as usual, played a gangster.) He compared his feelings that night to the experience of St. Paul on the road to Damascus: epiphanous. "The soaps have become life," he piped. It was no longer possible to tell where one stopped and the other started.[11]

As a founding member of the American Federation of Radio Artists (*Hard Times*, 10) and the owner of such a distinctive voice, Terkel had little trouble landing parts. Everyone needed crooks. The problem was keeping jobs. His characters, after brief dramatic runs, were always being sent away to prison or shot dead. "My tenure," he said in *Working: People Talk about What They Do All Day* (1974), "was as uncertain as that of a radical college professor" (xvi). Hoping for longer runs, he developed, in addition to his gangster voice, an all-purpose "foreign" accent: his ability to play Russians, Germans, "Mediterraneans," and even "Levantines" made him a bit more versatile. No one, not even his various directors, seemed to notice that his various foreign voices were identical.

But "foreigners" in 1930s radio dramas were usually up to as little good as gangsters, and they too were likely to be caught and either sent away or shot. Either way, Terkel's parts tended to be short. In frustration, not to say desperation, he once begged a director to cast him as a leading man – someone respectable, with a longer life expectancy – but he was told that heroes had pear-shaped tones and that his tones were apricot-shaped (*Talking*, 150).

In *Talking to Myself: A Memoir of My Times* (1977) Terkel emphasized that, despite his early exposure to criminal elements on the streets of Chicago and his later success at playing crooks on radio, he was never in real life personally involved in crime. "My experience as a paid killer, safe cracker, and extortionist was, alas, ersatz," he wrote. "I was a soap opera villain" (*Talking*, 149). Yet he seems to have relished being a drugstore mobster, and he played it both on radio and in real life. He was in fact playing it the night in 1938 when he met the woman he would marry the next year, Ida Goldberg.

Ida and some of her friends were standing in the lobby of a Chicago theater, discussing a play they had heard was showing in

New York. A small man with an upturned collar, his face shaded by a large hat brim and his voice that of a small-time hoodlum, shouldered his way into their conversation. He told them all about the play, which he may or may not have seen, and invited himself to join their party.[12]

Ida, who was a social worker, had a keen eye for deception and almost immediately penetrated his disguise. But she found his act, if not his name, charming. She joined him later for coffee. As they got to know each other, she was impressed by the way his eyes sparkled when he spoke of literature, the theater, and liberal social causes. They had the same interests and ideals: she loved the theater and the New Deal and would soon stop wearing silk stockings to protest Japanese militarism in Asia. She married Terkel on 2 April 1939. At the time he owed her $20, but she insists he did not marry her to pay off interest on the loan.

Times were uncertain when Studs and Ida married. The depression lingered. War was coming. Terkel landed a radio show of his own, a 15-minute commentary on the news in the manner of the then-popular H. V. Kaltenborn. But in 1940 Terkel took chances by criticizing Colonel McCormick. A man from Aurora, as he was buying $500 worth of clothing from Terkel's sponsor, happened to mention how much he enjoyed the way Terkel put the old colonel in his place. The sponsor, who apparently never listened to Terkel, was appalled to learn that he was paying the salary of a man who dared to challenge the great man, and he sent Terkel packing. "Who am I to challenge Colonel McCormick?" Terkel asked himself philosophically as he cleaned out his desk (*Talking*, 43).

For a time he and Ida had to live on her salary, but in 1941 Terkel returned to the Federal Writers Project, earning $94 a month. He was working at the FWP when Pearl Harbor was attacked, and in early 1942, almost 30, he was called up for military duty. He was a soldier for only a bit more than a year. While he did not file as a conscientious objector, as he first planned to do, he did ask to work for the Red Cross but was turned down. He went to basic training, where he was found to be unfit for active duty because of a perforated eardrum, and was assigned to Special Services as an entertainer. From camp to camp, in Missouri, Colorado, and North Carolina, he led a band of musicians and actors, serving as their emcee and Dutch uncle. He wore the three stripes of a sergeant.[13]

He was the old guy among boys, the "avuncular one to the man-children." Because he had been a radical in the 1930s, he now found himself being spied on by a host of government agents. Much later, thanks to the Freedom of Information Act, he was able to look at the files they kept on him while he lived in army barracks. He found that he was judged a nice enough fellow who nevertheless needed watching. He was considered probably a loyal American, despite his outspoken views on equal rights for "coloreds" (Katz, 3).

Radio and Television

Mustered out of army duty and back home in Chicago by 1943, Terkel was hired by the Myerhoff Agency to write a series of patriotic radio scripts called "Great Americans." The programs were aired on Colonel McCormick's WGN, whose call letters stood for World's Greatest Newspaper, referring to his *Chicago Tribune.* By September 1945, when the war ended, Terkel had worked his way into a disc jockey's slot on station WCFL. He later admitted that at the time of Hiroshima and Nagasaki he felt no guilt or sadness, that he was just glad to see the war end, by whatever means (Koch, 84). It was much later that he came to feel differently about the use of the atomic bomb.

By late 1945 he was well enough established in radio broadcasting, both as a writer and as a performer, that the manager of WENR, I. J. Wagner, let him create his own show. "Studs Terkel's Wax Museum" featured recordings by and conversations with jazz and folk musicians, a format he has used ever since. This was the first time Chicago had heard the music Terkel played offered as authentic, legitimate works of art. The folk music he played was still considered by most urbanites to be either "cowboy" or "hillbilly." The jazz was still considered "race music." Without apology, indeed with pride, Terkel served up big helpings of Burl Ives, the Weavers, Bill Broonzy, and Memphis Minnie.

He still had to buy the recordings of black musicians at street stands in Hyde Park, though, because they were not available in shops or from mail-order companies. At one such stand in 1944 he had run across a record by a female gospel singer, new to him, named Mahalia Jackson. He was fascinated by her voice and her

energy, played her records on his new show, and was given credit
for "discovering" her. In point of fact – as he himself was always
quick to say – all he really did was introduce her to a wider audience
than the one that had already discovered her. When after some
months of playing her records on the air he finally went to hear her
sing at the Greater Salem Baptist Church, he realized that she had
long before been "discovered" by her own people.

Terkel and Jackson became fast friends. They spent long hours
together talking about music, and they appeared together on the
concert stage. At one concert he was so caught up in the emotion of
her song "A City Called Heaven" that he missed his next cue. "I was
pole-axed," he explained to her after the show (*Talking*, 113). Jackson later hired Terkel to write her television show and refused to fire
him when the Communist hunters were dogging his steps. Though
she never quite succeeded, despite all her friendly efforts, to get
Terkel "saved" from hell, Terkel still says that if anyone could have
done it, it would have been Jackson.

With the success of his radio show, Terkel became a recognized
figure in Chicago. The *Sun-Times* hired him to be its folk and jazz
music critic, and he began to emcee more and more concerts. He
even went on tour with a program that played to college crowds over
a broad swatch of the Midwest. Called "I Come for to Sing," it featured Bill Broonzy on blues, Win Stracke on frontier music, and
Larry Lane on Elizabethan ballads. Terkel himself steered clear of
singing – he has what he calls a "split-tenor" voice, which means he
cannot carry a tune – but under his direction the other three talented men demonstrated the way certain themes and even musical
forms have found their way into the songs of every age and race. A
photograph of this happy band, looking contented if not particularly
prosperous, appears in Terkel's book *Chicago* (104).

Terkel was a busy man in the late 1940s, doing all the things he
loved best. He was both an entertainer and an educator, surrounded
by music of all kinds, recognized and respected for his energy,
curiosity, and expertise. The hectic schedule he followed honed his
critical faculties and toughened him for the hard times that lay just
ahead. As Nelson Algren said, these days on the road and on the go
trained Terkel in the skills of a prairie dog: how to dig several holes
in which to hide from predators. If one were blocked, he could head
for another (Koch, 84). He was about to need them.

As the 1940s ended, however, the clouds were not yet on the Chicago horizon. Terkel was in fact making a move to the promising new medium of television. Chicago was primed to be a pioneer city for television, as it had been for radio, and Terkel the radio entertainer was there at the creation. He was financially comfortable and immensely popular. He had a reputation for taking chances and was considered a bit eccentric (he had emceed a fiftieth birthday celebration for Paul Robeson), but Chicago liked him, applauded his daring, and forgave his occasional radical gesture.

In 1949 he had played a bartender on an NBC television series called "Saturday Squares" and was judged a natural for the new medium. In 1950 he was asked by Biggy Levin, who had produced the successful Chicago-based shows "Kukla, Fran, and Ollie" and "Dave Garroway," to expand his bartender role and lead the cast of a show of his own. Garroway's scriptwriter Charlie Andrews offered the format: a bar where guests would drop by each week, talk about current events, and sing their songs, all mixed into themes chosen by Terkel himself. "Studs' Place" made its debut on NBC television in the fall of 1950.

"Studs' Place" epitomized what has been called Television Chicago Style. It was low-key, spontaneous, intimate. The Chicago style was eventually buried by the fast, slick, cool styles of New York and Los Angeles, but there are still some critics who regret that the old Chicago form did not triumph, or at least survive as an alternative to the standard fare. There were no written scripts for "Studs' Place," just outlines and rehearsal discussions of the topics to be explored and the songs to be sung the next week. The first year's run was a resounding success, and after Terkel suspended production in 1951 in order to tour with Chester Morris in Sidney Kingsley's play *Detective Story*, "Studs' Place" reappeared, this time not as a bar but as a barbecue restaurant. The format continued to be informal, conversational, and entertaining, Terkel's eternal trademarks (Koch, 85).

"Studs' Place," as conceived and executed, was "true to life." "Brecht would have roared" at it, Terkel says, remembering how it offered each week a slice of real life. Terkel and his colleagues envisioned an Eden, he now admits, naively believing that television would be a vehicle for humanism. As it turned out, television rapidly descended into the netherworld of commercial aridity. Content bowed to form, truth to profit, man to mammon.[14] The idealist in

Terkel was disenchanted as much as the entertainer in him was frustrated.

For a couple of years Terkel and his troupe enjoyed a national audience, small as such audiences were in those days. He kept a regular cast of characters: restaurant pianist Chet Robel, good buddy Win Stracke as a guitar-strumming hobo, actress Bev Younger as the waitress Gracie, and, of course, Terkel as proprietor and resident philosopher. Nelson Algren and other writers came by to share their wisdom. Mahalia Jackson first appeared on television as a visitor to Terkel's beanery. The show's success, Terkel believes, lay in its willingness to portray life as ordinary people, the viewers, knew it to be. He received letters of approval from every part of the nation and from all classes of people. The show seemed so real to its viewers that 30 years after it left the air Terkel would still be asked, "What ever happened to that restaurant you used to have?" (Koch, 85).

Terkel was completely committed to the show. At one point during its run he was called to New York for an interview with Billy Rose, who asked him to help him create a new show, but Terkel purposely botched the interview so that he could get back to Chicago and his "Place." He still has fantasies about the television career he might have had, about how he and his show might have made television better. In a sense his oral histories are simply later episodes of "Studs' Place." In each of them Terkel chooses performers, provides them with an outline, and lets them make up their own lines. If not television, then literature.

"Red"

The fatalist in Terkel says that "Studs' Place" was too good to last, while the optimist in him says that what happened was all for the best. What ended "Studs' Place" was not any loss of inspiration or diminution of talent but the advent of the Red Scare.

In 1950 Senator Joseph McCarthy of Wisconsin started a crusade to track down and exterminate every vestige of the American liberalism left over from the depression's New Deal and the wartime collaboration with the Soviet Union. Terkel had been a liberal, perhaps a radical, in the 1930s. He had served his country during the war, but he was known still to believe in social, economic, and racial justice, all of which were now suspect. He was, although his detractors never mentioned it publicly, a Jew. He was a sitting duck.

On 10 October 1952 one Owen Vincent told the House Un-American Activities Committee (HUAC) in Los Angeles that during the 1930s Studs Terkel had invited him to join the Communist party. The HUAC apparently did not take this testimony too seriously, because it neither subpoenaed Terkel to testify nor pursued the matter further (Koch, 85). On the other hand, the HUAC made no attempt to refute the charges or to put the matter to rest. Terkel was not a government official or employee, no security risk, and the HUAC could be reasonably certain that the entertainment establishment would keep its plate clean.

Indeed, NBC's executives told Terkel publicly to disavow the accusation and assure the media that he had outgrown his youthful liberalism – in other words, to make an apology for his radical opinions and to refrain from further statements or acts that might provoke his critics. Terkel refused. From that point he was regularly identified in newspaper articles as "Studs Terkel, the Red radio actor." He was placed on the blacklist. "Studs' Place" fell victim to the hysteria.

NBC gave several lame excuses for dropping the show. The coffee company that sponsored it had complained that the show was not attracting new viewers, not expanding its original market base. Hollywood studios were able to produce variety shows of wider appeal at less cost. Chicago-style television was just not commercially competitive with New York television and future demands in the medium. Terkel's viewers and loyal fans protested the decision to cancel the show with letters and telephone calls, but the decision was final. Although ABC picked up the show for a brief time in 1953, it was carried by only a limited number of outlets in a few cities and after this brief revival was finally laid to rest.

Terkel says that this was the low point in his long career. He tried two new radio shows, "The Voice of the Terkel" and "Sound of the City," the latter on Sterling (Red) Quinlan's ABC affiliate WBKB. It was a midnight show, and on it Terkel and his cohort Vincent de Paul Garrity moved about Chicago, capturing the sounds of their town by night. But the Red label stuck to Terkel, and eventually each show was canceled, as were his contract with the *Sun-Times* and a number of personal appearances (*Talking*, 51), all because rumor had it that he was a Communist. Most of the rumors were manufactured by a Chicago florist named Ed Clamage.

Clamage (whose name is spelled in various accounts as "Clammage" and even "Klamisch") was chairman of the Anti-Subversion Committee of one of Chicago's American Legion posts – a Jewish one, incidentally – and used his position to hunt for liberals to tag as Communists. In Terkel he found a perfect target, and he pursued him with a vengeance. He sent copies of the Owen Vincent HUAC testimony to radio and television stations, newspapers, and even presidents of clubs that had public affairs speakers, warning sponsors and executives of the risk they took dealing with a man of Studs Terkel's unsavory reputation.

It is perplexing to see the way supposedly responsible men, some of them known as courageous journalists and public servants, caved in to the minor-league pressures of a man like Clamage. His crusade killed any chances of a revival for "Studs' Place," cost Terkel his two radio jobs, and even took away several pending offers of other jobs. Clamage dogged his every step for months, even to the point of calling groups before which Terkel was already scheduled to speak, pressuring them to cancel his engagements, robbing him of much-needed income (Koch, 85). Clamage even tried, in vain it seems, to have Terkel dismissed from a night-class teaching assignment at the University of Chicago. Even Clamage's ridiculous excesses, such as his attack on the Girl Scouts for selling cookies to aid the "subversive" UNICEF, were taken seriously.

Terkel once estimated that during 1952-53 the Clamage crusade cost him 65 percent of his potential income, yet he never showed the slightest bitterness toward his nemesis. He was able to remain calm amid the storm and avoid personal recrimination by recognizing that Clamage was merely an instrument of a national disease, one he refused to let infect him. Terkel even seemed to take a perverse delight in all the attention he was receiving. He maintained his usual buoyancy and laughed at Clamage and his rage. He saved all of his anger for Clamage's false patriotism, refusing to waste it on personal vindictiveness.

Terkel's good-natured reaction to the campaign to discredit him proved to be the best-possible choice. He outlived both Clamage and the crusade and eventually won back all and more than he had lost. At one point, when Clamage tried to pressure a group to withdraw its invitation for Terkel to speak, his fee jumped from $100 to $200, and Terkel promptly wrote Clamage a note, detailing his good luck and offering him a $10 agent's fee. Every time you attack me, he teased, my salary goes up. When Clamage died of a heart attack three days later, Terkel boasted, "I killed the guy" (Terry, 9). "Poor Clamage," he joked, "has gone to the Great American Legion Post in the sky" (Fitzpatrick, 2).

Terkel got some help during these bad years from a friend in broadcasting, Red Quinlan. In his memoirs he would praise Quinlan for taking risks for him, describing him as radio's equivalent of a wide-ranging, devil-may-care baseball shortstop. For a brief time, with Quinlan's help, Terkel hosted a local television omnibus show called "Briefcase." For a bit longer he did a radio show called "Breaking the News." Little came of either program, except that they kept Terkel's name before the public. He continued to speak before clubs and organizations, most of them labor-based, and he continued to emcee benefit concerts – one of them, oddly enough, chaired by a sister of Ed Clamage. He spent more time than in previous years with his young son Paul. He began collecting materials for a book of short biographies of jazz musicians.

Throughout the 1950s, however, Terkel was under FBI surveillance. Agents called him on the telephone at all hours and felt free to drop by his home to ask him questions. Terkel found these men to be thoroughly humorless, a bit sad, but relatively harmless. Again he refused to be angry with individuals. The first time they came to his home Ida was so incensed that she ordered Terkel to kick them out. But the diminutive master of the house had a better plan. He invited them to sit down, offered them drinks, and gave them a lecture on Henry David Thoreau and the virtues of civil disobedience: in short, killed them with kindness and gab. The bewildered, frustrated agents finally gave up and left. The last telephone call they made, however, caught Terkel in a foul mood because he had just broken a valuable phonograph record, and he took his revenge. He pretended to think that the agent was a friend playing a prank, fumed and cursed at him in a good-natured way, and warned the man not to try to trick old Studs that way again. In confusion the agent conceded defeat and hung up, never to call again (*Talking*, 128-29).

Slowly both the accusations of disloyalty and the FBI harassment died away, and Terkel prevailed. When much later he reflected on that period of his life, he concluded that he had actually been lucky. He was fortunate not to have lived on either coast. The Chicago media, while callous, were comparatively easy on him. Chicago journalists apparently did not take Clamage and his kind seriously, and they declined to use Terkel to sell papers. On either the East or West Coast, Terkel allowed, he would have been slaughtered (Terry, 8).

Facetiously yet convincingly, Terkel has also argued that had he not been blacklisted he would not have had free time to indulge his latent fantasy about writing a book. During the slack time of the rumors he began research on the work that would in time become *Giants of Jazz*, which in turn would lead to his other books and to his international fame. "Hell, if I hadn't been blacklisted," he has said, "I would never have written either *Division Street* or *Hard Times*" (Fitzpatrick, 8). To those can now be added *Working*, *Talking to Myself*, *American Dreams: Lost and Found* (1980), *"The Good War": An Oral History of World War II* (1984), *Chicago, The Great Divide: Second Thoughts on the American Dream*, and *Race: How Blacks and Whites Think and Feel about the American Obsession* (1992).

He has also mused that had he not been kicked out of television when he was, he might have been persuaded to move to New York and host a network late-night talk show in the style of Jack Paar. There he would have either let himself slide into intellectual sloth or rebelled against it and asked the wrong person an impertinent question and been fired. Either way, he believes, he would have come to a bad end (Katz, 3).

In his memoirs he speculated that had he heeded the advice of the network executives and toned down his radical opinions, he might have become a tame, closet liberal. With his law degree, literary skills, and knack at manipulating the media, he might have become a Henry Kissinger type of government official, proved Alger Hiss and Julius and Ethel Rosenberg guilty of subversion, and become editor of journals for the CIA. At the end of this speculation, with a twinkle so bright it carried over into print, he sighed, "Oh well . . ." (*Talking*, 125).

Whatever the plethora of theoretical scenarios, Terkel is quite content to have sacrificed them all for the life he has led. He survived the McCarthy era with his health, integrity, and optimism intact, perhaps even more self-assured than before, certainly smarter, and went on to become the Studs Terkel millions of people admire. For all this his fans echo his refrain: "Long live the blacklist!" (Katz, 3).

Hope

During the days Lillian Hellman called "rascal time," the days of the Red witch-hunt and the blacklist, gospel singer Mahalia Jackson remained one of Terkel's stalwart friends. She repaid the help Terkel had given her along the way with interest. She hired him as a writer for her CBS radio show and stood guard to protect him from his detractors. The time Terkel was "pole-axed" by Jackson's song about heaven and forgot his next line, she teased him, "I know Studs ain't a believer, but if I could save him . . ." And Terkel, having regained his composure, replied, "Baby, I'm beyond salvation, but if anybody could do it you're the one" (*Talking*, 113). Though he would later admit that with her music she demolished the most intricate arguments for atheism, in the end "even Mahalia failed" to get him saved.

Yet one hears strong echoes of Jackson's theology in the way Terkel speaks. While he remains an ethnic Jew and an agnostic, if not a true atheist, his speeches are liberally sprinkled with religious, even Christian, references and themes. It is as if by listening so long and faithfully to Jackson he absorbed some of her faith. Spiritually, perhaps unconsciously, Terkel is just a bit of a black Baptist.

At one point when Terkel was writing for Jackson's show, CBS president William Paley issued an order that all network employees must sign the national loyalty oath and cease all public social criticism. As in the earlier case with his own show, Terkel refused to compromise with what he considered right-wing blackmail, and again he was fired. Jackson was both furious and adamant: "If Studs don't write the show, Mahalia don't sing," she told Paley.[15] CBS got the message. Terkel continued to write the show; he neither signed the oath nor softened his opinions.

Their friendship was not without pain, however. In his memoirs Terkel describes the sad night he realized that, because she was black, Jackson could not dine with him at the restaurant across the street from their studio (*Talking*, 265-66). At her funeral he had to sit in stunned silence as Richard Daley presided and black dancer Sammy Davis, Jr., briefly appeared at the podium and read a letter of condolence from his good friend Richard Nixon. For Terkel, having such men eulogize his friend was the ultimate sacrilege.[16]

In 1954, as Joe McCarthy was investigating the army and precipitating the televised demise of his own crusade, Terkel happened to tune in to a Chicago radio station that immediately captured his interest and imagination. It was WFMT, a small, fledgling "culture" FM station, then only three years old, that featured an odd mixture of classical and folk music. The first voice he heard was that of Woody Guthrie. He was so intrigued that he dropped by the studio and asked for a job (McBride, 4).

Terkel was already an experienced, knowledgeable, popular figure about Chicago. He had obvious strengths and weaknesses. He would attract listeners, but he would also attract controversy. WFMT's program director, Bernard Jacobs, needed Terkel's assets and chose to overlook his liabilities. He set his new disc jockey up in a daily music and talk show, at first called "Studs Terkel's Wax Museum," like the earlier one, and then after it was syndicated "Studs Terkel's Almanac." Terkel played jazz, folk, and the classics. He interviewed composers and performers. He learned the skills that later made him an oral historian.

Terkel and WFMT were made for each other. Within five years his show had won first place in Ohio State University's ratings of nationwide cultural radio programs. The show was syndicated to the nation's large cities and beamed by cable to smaller outlets. It made Terkel famous and the station rich. It introduced Terkel to an audience large, wide, and faithful enough to make the oral histories he produced best-sellers.

WFMT became Terkel's home. He has hung his hat there for almost 40 years.

Chapter Two

A Grand Inquisitor

Studs Terkel has been a regular feature of WFMT for many years. A white man who plays black music, an urban man who plays folk, an agnostic who plays gospel, a regular guy who plays the classics – he is unique. Playing all that music led Terkel to interviews and friendships with composers and performers. Interviews and friendships led to books. By 1989 WFMT (98.7) was one of the nation's great media success stories, and "Studs Terkel's Almanac" was its most valued and respected program.

Until October 1988 the hour-long "Almanac" aired at 11:00 A.M. weekdays, with the past week's best show repeated at 10:30 P.M. on Thursdays. Terkel said modestly that his large audience was composed mostly of urban and suburban housewives who listened mostly out of habit, but in fact his audiences – nationwide because of syndication – have always cut across social boundaries. In 1988 the show, in the Chicago area, was moved to 5:30 P.M. daily, "drive time," with no diminution of appeal.[1]

WFMT's president and general manager, Ray Nordstrand, who succeeded Bernard Jacobs in 1968, himself known as something of an eccentric radio man, immediately recognized the valuable commodity he had in the eccentric Terkel, gave him a free rein, and watched him grow. He understood that Terkel was no dispassionate, objective observer of events and people; that he had strong, activist opinions; and that he was at his best when he expressed them. His style was free association, nonlinear, and it was better for all concerned not to hold him to traditional formulas, in either his choice of music or method of interviewing. Terkel actually read the books and truly listened to the music he featured on his show; it was only right that he should be deeply involved in what their authors had to say. Nordstrand let Terkel play to his strengths and forgave his various weaknesses (Terry, 8).

Jim Unrath, who served for many years as Terkel's main operating director, early recognized that Terkel had no mechanical skills. Unrath compensated by assuming complete technical responsibility for the show. He saw that in a certain way Terkel's inability to handle equipment was actually an advantage, as it tended to be charming and to put guests at ease, and so he made no attempt to improve Terkel's skills. Lois Baum, associate program director, worked most closely with Terkel and early learned to make allowances for his eccentricities. He had to be the center of attention, even when interviewing or featuring someone else, or he grew bored. He also needed strong guests, people who would not give in to him, who would balance his strong opinions, who would even challenge him – and these she provided. Cathy Zmuda, who became Terkel's personal assistant, transcribed the miles of taped interviews he made into typescript for his oral histories. Each 1 April she would appear, tongue-in-cheek, as "Candy Armstrong-Jones," a denizen of suburban "Sandburg Village," a housewife and the author of two soft-porn novels, *City of Sin* and *Village of Vice.* Her death in the late 1980s was a personal blow to Terkel (Terry, 7).

There have been changes at WFMT over the years – and a few crises. In 1968 Jacobs sold the station to Tribune Broadcasting, and within two years there were problems. A "Citizens Committee to Save WFMT" challenged the new management, which was bent on making changes the staff opposed. Chicago's WTTW-TV, channel 11, acting as peacemaker between the factions, assumed control of the station later that year. But by 1985 more troubles arose, this time between WFMT and channel 11. A new chief at channel 11, John Diedrichs, wanted to streamline management, removing Nordstrand, in order to make the station more profitable.

Calling the plan "obscenely unfair" and proclaiming, "We're in the eighth circle of hell," Terkel entered the fray. When Diedrichs responded to Terkel's complaints about "plantation-style management" by suggesting that it might be time for Terkel to retire, the old disc jockey yelled that he would never do that, that he would have to be fired, knowing, of course, that he was a Chicago icon and that firing him would be a public relations nightmare for channel 11.[2] The controversy goes on still, as management brings in what Terkel calls "canned ads" to make the station show a 15 rather than the old 5 percent profit margin. Terkel says the staff is terrified and the quality in a state of decline. Younger people are being fired; older ones are being slapped with a gag rule.

By 1990 a similar problem had arisen at Terkel's publishing house, Pantheon, a division of Random House. A new management, failing to recognize the prestige value of Pantheon, called for higher profit margins there, pressured its staff, and forced the resignation of its editor André Schiffrin, who had introduced Terkel to the literary world. Terkel flew to New York and helped picket the company, threatening to take his books elsewhere. And he did: his next book, *Race*, appeared under the imprint of the publishing house Schiffrin founded when he left Pantheon, The New Press. All this trouble, merely for profit, Terkel groused; "the two most obscene words in the English language are 'bottom line.'"[3]

Some Jazz Giants

Terkel finally completed the book on jazz musicians that he had begun during the lean late 1940s as he was starting his work with WFMT. *Giants of Jazz* (1957), which details the lives and achievements of 13 jazz musicians, opened up a new career for Terkel. He drew on information he had gained from interviews and conversations with these musicians and their friends to interpret and critique the work of the men and women, mostly black, who created the music he so dearly loved.

Dedicated to the memory of John Lewellen and in appreciation of Elizabeth Riley, *Giants* was an ambitious undertaking, even though it proved a thin volume. Terkel gave each musician a chapter and each chapter a title: the musician's name and a descriptive phrase to help identify his or her place in the world of jazz. Joe Oliver is simply "The King." Louis Armstrong is dubbed "Ambassador of Jazz." To Bessie Smith he gives the title "Empress of the Blues." Bix Beiderbeck, one of three whites included, is "Young Man with a Horn." Fats Waller is the "Laughing Genius." Duke Ellington is the man who gave America the "Sounds of Life." Benny Goodman, who enlarged the popularity of jazz by bringing it to a predominantly white audience, is "King of Swing." The command of Count Basie's music is "Jump for Joy." Beside Billie Holiday's name is the prayerful phrase "God Bless the Child." Woody Herman is

"Leader of the Herd." Dizzy Gillespie is "Explorer of New Sounds."
Charlie Parker is "Yardbird." At the end of the list, with John
Coltrane, Terkel merely says, "The Search Continues."

Giants sold well. Eighteen years after it was published it was still
enough in demand to be reissued. The second edition, produced
with the help of Milly Hawk Daniel, was larger than the first and contained photographs of the featured artists.

The book has unquestioned merit. From Terkel's fertile imagination and gift for description come colorful scenes from the lives of
the artists. Some of these scenes are, of course, fictional, even
though they are built around actual people, places, and events;
readers should remember that the scenes are meant only to
approximate reality. Readers should also keep in mind that no matter
how familiar a white writer is with black culture and the processes
through which black music is produced, he cannot know for sure
that he has captured the essence of black life and thought. Terkel
boldly assumes in *Giants* that he does understand such things and
moves without hesitation into his sweeping interpretations.

He is at his best here when he describes the struggles that were
so much a part of his musicians' climb to fame, perhaps because he
knew from personal experience this side of the artist's life. In each
story there are recurring themes: early poverty and emotional priva-
tion; sudden breaks with family, friends, and lovers over addiction to
music and its demands; the debilitating effects of travel, loneliness,
alcohol, and even financial success. This pattern of struggle to success to tragedy provides Terkel with his theme and his thesis. Its
repetition does become at times monotonous and makes it hard for
readers to distinguish one life from another as Terkel's subjects
travel their common road, but it makes its point.

Despite some flaws, however, this first Terkel book is a significant one, for in it he treated these "giants" not as celebrities of the
stage and screen variety but as human beings with human dreams,
joys, weaknesses, and sorrows. He gave jazz a greater cultural weight
than it had previously known by providing it with a historical setting
and demonstrating its broad musical influence. He introduced his
giants and their music to a new audience, one that had not been
acquainted with jazz during the early years of rock, thereby gratifying
jazz's old fans and winning it new ones.

Terkel saved for the end, after the biographies, his definition of jazz and his evaluation of its merits. In his own peculiarly vivid style he explained that jazz is a spicy mixture of all the American cultural, social, and ethnic ingredients: "It was to America the Black came from West Africa – on the slave ship – bringing with him his complex and exciting rhythms. It was to America the European came, bringing with him his folk songs, dances, and marches. The Black American absorbed these melodies and added to them his rhythms. Also he added the deep feeling of his spirituals and the bone strength of his work songs."[4] Despite the stereotypical portrait of the black as a person with natural rhythm whose forms need white content for completion, this theory of jazz put the subject before a new public and initiated intellectual discussions of a musical form that is indeed a synthesis of black and white cultural patterns, born on this continent of emotions enhanced by dreams of freedom.

Public Man

Studs Terkel the public man is both an entertainer and a man of letters, intensely curious about music, literature, philosophy, and politics. His personality is effervescent and irrepressible, and his mind forms opinions on every subject he explores. He has hardly an unspoken thought. His voice, his face, his hair, and even the way he dresses contribute to an image that attracts, captures, and convinces large audiences.

His distinctive costume, which Ida calls "the uniform," started to take form in 1963, when Terkel saw a man at a party wearing a red-checkered shirt. He admired it so much that Ida bought him one like it. To the shirt he added, over the years, a red knit necktie worn loosely, red socks, charcoal-gray trousers with gray Hush Puppies, and a navy blue blazer. In winter he adds a red sweater and a red scarf. The uniform never varies.

The redness has raised a few eyebrows. Some of his detractors have said that he dresses according to his political persuasion. In Britain, where members of the Labour party proudly wear red roses and neckties during campaigns, this would be no insult; in America, with our history of Red scares and Red-baiting, it is. Terkel counters his critics by saying that red is the color of life, the color of compassion. He sometimes calls himself Will Scarlet, after Robin Hood's follower, one of the merry men who robbed the rich to feed the poor, and he likes to point out that Italian unification leader Garibaldi wore red to signify that he was on the side of truth. To those brave enough to suggest to Terkel's face that his red duds are a sign of Communist sympathies, he gives the well-known Chicago reply, a favorite of former Mayor Daley, "Go screw yourself" (Galloway, 8). Terkel does not, however, say such things on national television, as did Daley during the Democratic National Convention in 1968.

A steady job on the radio and a new career as a writer did not slow Terkel's public life as he entered his fifth decade. In a four-year span he acted in four Chicago productions of nationally successful stage plays. After playing the part of George in the stage version of John Steinbeck's short novel *Of Mice and Men,* he went on in 1958 to portray Eddie Carbone in Arthur Miller's *A View from the Bridge.* At the end of this play Eddie is stabbed and dies dramatically, courageously, and purposefully. Terkel relished the role and played it with grace, skill, and dignity.

The next year, keeping up his steady pace, Terkel starred in Moss Hart's comedy *Light up the Sky* as Sidney Black, one of several actors trying to make it big on Broadway. Although this play provided Terkel with less opportunity to demonstrate his dramatic skills, it appealed to him because it permitted him to do comedy. He proved to be as effective a comic as he had been a dramatic actor, and as he had been a radio gangster.

In 1960, nearing his fiftieth year, Terkel played perhaps the most demanding and rewarding, certainly the most appropriate role of his stage career in the Chicago production of William Saroyan's *The Cave Dwellers.* As the King of Tramps he played opposite actress-director Mme Eugenie Leontovich, who had played the same part in the New York production of 1957. This is not, of course, Saroyan's best play. Set in the depression, featuring a group of social outcasts gathered for shelter in an old theater condemned and ready to be demolished, it seemed to audiences of the affluent late 1950s and early 1960s woefully out of date. It was said to be old-fashioned and sentimental, long on characterization and short on story, and was dismissed for its lack of suspense.

Terkel knew, of course, that it was not dated, that there were countless outcasts and misfits in Eisenhower's America. He loved Saroyan's characters, both the ones he put on the stage and the ones out across the country that they represented. He was himself perfectly cast as the King of Tramps, and the words he delivered when someone asked him why the world was made could just as well have come from his own pen as from Saroyan's: "What is the world for? It's for putting up with . . . with humor, if possible. Without excuses, without astonishment, without regret, without shame, without any system and order more elaborate than courtesy and love."

Hand in hand with acting, Terkel continued to serve as master of ceremonies for concerts, and to these he added festivals – the Ravinia Music Festival, the Chicago Folk Festival, and the Newport Folk Festival. These popular appearances enlarged Terkel's personal following, introduced him to new musicians and their music, and helped stock his radio show with more and better interviews than he had previously been able to manage and afford.

He even had a brief fling as a playwright. In 1959 he wrote a contemporary tragicomedy called *Amazing Grace*, about an Irish-American family trying to survive their own hard times. It was read by friends but essentially gathered dust until 1967, when it was staged in December by the Professional Theater Program at the University of Michigan, funded by a special grant of $25,000 from the National Council on the Arts. In the program notes Terkel called the play "my quarrel with a cool antagonist, indifference. The air of impersonality pervades our society. I find this appalling and terrifying. I suppose you might call the play both a cry and a warning. A cry for help – help to feel. A warning that Orwell may be just around the corner." On the visual plane, he said, the play was about an elderly woman and her two sons, "One being her true passionate nature, the other her contemporary pose." Beyond the visual, however, his audience might see the two sides of modern society.[5]

Amazing Grace was generally well received, but it did not move beyond the cushioned, open-minded, sophisticated university setting. It was Terkel's first and last play. At various times his oral histories have been successfully adapted for the stage, but he has let other men do the honors. He is more gifted as an actor than as a playwright and more gifted as an oral historian than as an actor. This is a judgment, however, that he will not make and receives without pleasure.

In the 1960s Terkel made several trips that broadened his horizons considerably. In 1962 he visited Britain and Italy. In Britain he interviewed Lord Bertrand Russell, and in Italy, where he received the Prix d'Italia, he interviewed film director Vittorio De Sica. The following year, because, much to his amusement, he was considered a prominent "midwestern journalist," he was invited on Lufthansa German Airlines' maiden flight from Frankfurt to Johannesburg and spent two weeks in South Africa. There he interviewed both blacks and whites, servants as well as masters, and returned to the United States convinced that apartheid must end. The South African police, enforcers of the system, reminded him of the Chicago police of the 1920s – and of police in the American South as late as 1963 (*Talking*, 114).

Back at home Terkel became ever more interested in civil rights and the politics of desegregation. In August 1963 he rode a freedom train to and from Washington to attend the Lincoln Memorial rally where Martin Luther King, Jr., spoke and Mahalia Jackson sang. Along the way, as always, he interviewed participants in the great American drama. In 1965 he was in Selma, Alabama, for the March to Montgomery, interviewing people on both sides of the racial division. In 1968, closer to home, he interviewed participants in the conflagration surrounding the Democratic National Convention in Chicago. Each of these events taught him important lessons about the history, society, and personality of America and Americans and taught him how to compile oral histories.

The Tape Machine

Terkel began interviewing people, capturing their words and thoughts on wire and tape, for his radio shows. His first subjects were musicians. He talked with them about their work in order to create interest among his listeners, to explain music to them, and to satisfy their curiosity. He knew that his listeners were curious because he was curious. His first interview, with tenor saxophonist Bud Freeman, was conducted live on the radio around 1939. A decade later technology permitted Terkel to begin recording interviews, freeing him to conduct them when and where it was most convenient. As time passed he expanded his field of interest, and expertise, by interviewing writers and public figures as well as musicians. A tool for entertainment became a tool for education and then a tool for writing oral history. To write his oral histories Terkel would search out not just musicians, writers, and public figures but also America's elusive "common man."[6]

Terkel's first portable recorder was a German-made Uher; later he adopted a slightly more efficient Japanese-made Sony. Whatever make or style, he and his tape machines have now spent nearly half a century locked in an immensely productive and passionately stormy marriage of convenience. They have captured the deepest feelings, joys, and sorrows of twentieth-century American humanity, and without his companion he would not have been able to do so. He has said that he is himself more alive and imaginative when he presses the ON lever of his "mute companion." "I have a theory," he said. "I am a neo-Cartesian. I tape therefore I am" (*Talking,* 8).

It is a love-hate relationship. His recorder often refuses to cooperate. This was especially true in the early days, before cassettes, when Terkel used reels of tape. The machine would not start; it would unwind its tape into his lap; it would decide to unplug itself in the middle of an interview. Terkel would pound it, shake it, curse it gently. He still does, despite his recent models' greater efficiency. Although he seems at times to be blaming the machine, he admits when questioned about it that the fault lies mostly with him. "It's . . . I'm incompetent," he says (DeMott, 82). His colleagues at WFMT agree.

Terkel has always found machines a puzzle. His mechanical skills are as weak as his interpersonal ones are strong. He still finds it safer to take the 146 express bus between his home on the near north side and the radio station on Wacker Drive in the Loop than to try learning to drive himself (Terry, 7). He has never been able to ride a bicycle, roller-skate, dance, or perform any other activity that requires motor skills or physical dexterity and coordination. The tape recorder, as indispensable as it it for his work, is just another of the myriad instruments he cannot handle with grace.

There is, however, a beneficial element in his "incompetence," causing some people to believe that, if not intentional, it is at least studied. Terkel has interviewed more people on public transit and while being driven in cars than he would have been able to do had he been a driver himself. He understands quite well that when he and his machine are at odds, when he fumes at it and gives it a smack, the person he is interviewing begins to relax as the fear of relating intimate thoughts to a cold machine dissipates.[7] Neither Terkel nor his cantankerous friend is a threat, and so the words flow. Sometimes he even asks his subject to help him tame the awful contraption. It is "important to make a person feel needed," he says with a wink.

Ray Nordstrand compares Terkel the interviewer with Peter Falk's television detective Columbo, who works hard at being incompetent, plotting how to make foolish mistakes, in order to give suspects a false sense of security. Although Terkel is not pursuing criminals and his object is not incarceration, he is a tracker whose goal is to capture words. Nordstrand warns the unsuspecting prey that Terkel's incompetence should not be compared with that of Jacques Tati's Monsieur Hulot, with whom Terkel likes to compare himself. Whereas Monsieur Hulot is truly incapable of handling worldly matters, Terkel is simply a good actor (Terry, 7).

Terkel recognizes the value of his incompetence, real or feigned, in providing himself and his subjects with what he calls "mutual vulnerability" (Koch, 86). It makes for a good interview when someone sees that Terkel is just as common as he or she is. Terkel uses his clumsiness the way he uses his tousled, rumpled appearance, raffish voice, impish grin, comic gestures, and "near wordless garrulity" to good effect in selling himself.

After the successes of *Division Street, Hard Times: An Oral History of the Great Depression* (1970), *Working,* and *Talking to Myself,* a reporter asked Terkel during a press conference at New York's Algonquin Hotel whether his fame would limit his ability to get people to talk openly to him, whether the awe of speaking to a famous person and the knowledge that what is said could find its way into print might inhibit future subjects. Terkel answered no, not at all, because he would always be a klutz, which would keep him humble and put other people at ease.[8]

Once he relaxes his subject, Terkel seems to know instinctively what approach to take. He keeps the topic general and "improvises" the discussion. There are times, particularly when interviewing a public figure, that it is necessary to ask an impertinent question, even when doing so means angering the celebrity. Terkel believes that what scientist Jacob Bronowski once told him about the study of nature is true of people: at times the only way to get a pertinent answer is to ask an impertinent question (*Talking,* 239).

Such impertinence can extend to pressing people to continue their testimony even when they prefer to stop. At least Terkel has done this to his wife, Ida, and we can assume he has treated others the same way. Ida has appeared as "Eileen Barth" in a couple of the oral histories. Recalling for *Hard Times* a depression-era family's humiliation when they had to open a closet and show her their poverty, she once asked if she could take a break and have a cry. But Terkel, who wanted to capture her emotion, refused. The "old bastard made me go on," she says (Katz, 3).

Terkel has long been critical of network news interviews because he believes the interviewers lack the necessary impertinence to get at the truth. He often grouses that they never ask the real questions: the when, the why, the how questions (Grele, 19). In an article for the *Nation* he analyzed an ABC "Issues and Answers" interview with former Vietnam general and prisoner of war John Flynn. Not one of the reporters asked Flynn why the United States was in Vietnam. Not one challenged his claim that U.S. national objectives there were clearly understood. Not one asked how he knew the South Vietnamese government was stable and healthy.[9]

This was just two years before the South Vietnamese government collapsed and the glib statements about national objectives and purposes were shown to be false. With the fall of Saigon visible on the horizon, Terkel wrote another article for the *Nation* in which he encouraged young reporters to recover the muckraking style of early-twentieth-century journalists.[10] How much credit Terkel can take for the more aggressive, impertinent style of the new breed of television journalists that came along shortly thereafter – men like Ted Koppel and Sam Donaldson – is hard to say. But Terkel had by 1975 painted a vivid picture of telejournalism's weaknesses, and the new men have certainly tried to strengthen it.

Terkel knows how to be impertinent, and he has used his skill, particularly when interviewing a public figure. More often, however, he is sympathetic, or perhaps a better word is *empathetic*. Most of the time, when interviewing the common man, he invokes rather than provokes. He does not pursue questions that cause his subjects pain or force them to reveal intimacies they prefer to hide. André Schiffrin, his editor at Pantheon, says that Terkel uses the techniques of a boxer: "He knows when to feint, when to move away, when to hit. But there's no adversarial relationship." Terkel puts it more simply: "I'm a chameleon. I become the person" (Galloway, 1).

He is not always a smooth interviewer. He can be erratic, his mind jumping from one thing to another, too quickly for his subject. He does not always follow logical pathways. But his empathy usually saves him. He has compared himself as an interviewer to Billie Holiday as a singer. Though she never had the voice or the natural talent of Ella Fitzgerald, Holiday was open, bared herself fully, and was thus perhaps a better performer than Fitzgerald. Terkel says he may have less skill than other interviewers but is more open to the people he interviews. Robert Laing, a London psychiatrist, argues that for a counselor to help his patient he must be a "fellow-traveller" with him in the quest for health; he must share both his pain and his joy. Terkel is such a "fellow-traveler" with his guests (Koch, 86).

The result, according to Geoffrey Wolff in a review of *Hard Times,* is that "people talk miracles to Terkel. They'll confess anything to him." Among the things Terkel consistently draws from them, Wolff says, is the rarest gem of all, their "startling decency."[11] From the publication of his earliest oral histories questions have been raised about the way Terkel elicits his answers and whether he influences them, but no one doubts that the answers he gets from his subjects are startling.

No less a figure than John Kenneth Galbraith, in his review of *American Dreams* for *Saturday Review,* called Terkel the master of the interview. Galbraith suggested that Terkel had raised the interview from the level of journalistic and historical necessity to that of art. His secret? He *lets* his people talk; he does not *make* them talk. He clears the path for them without getting in their way. He makes it possible for them to express their deepest feelings in their own way without requiring them to do so.[12]

Raymond Schroth says that Terkel's success as an interviewer lies in his ability to accept his subjects' ultimate privacy. Terkel is willing to leave inviolate whatever core of being and experience the person being interviewed wishes to hide from him (Schroth, 381). By granting this most basic requests Terkel does indeed seem able to gain more from his witnesses than he would if he probed areas of intense intimacy.

Terkel says that he has no interest in asking personal questions, that his curiosity is intellectual, not prurient. He hints that this attitude stems from his own appreciation of how important it is to keep certain spaces enclosed. He is adamant that no one gain personal information from or about his son. He was more open with me before he learned that I was preparing a book on his life, and only after he assured himself that I would be dealing primarily with his public career did he resume his early familiarity. His unwillingness to trespass on private property, because he understands how it feels, makes Terkel one of the best questioners, best listeners, and best recorders of other people's words in America today.

From the beginning of his quest for the perfect interview, Terkel has preferred the common to the famous. While he has interviewed – mostly for the radio but also for his books – a number of celebrities, the "little people" on his list far outnumber the big ones (McBride, 4). Like Bertolt Brecht, one of his heroes, Terkel is fond of the saying that the pharaohs did not build the pyramids that bear their names – and that had he been there he would have interviewed day laborers. Julius Caesar did not conquer Gaul, and Terkel says he would have interviewed foot soldiers. Francis Drake did not sink the Spanish Armada, and Terkel would have interviewed sailors, as he could not have interviewed the wind. Had he been at the foot of Calvary that Friday – which is his grandest dream – he would have interviewed bystanders about "that subversive on the cross."[13]

Benjamin DeMott, who has observed Terkel at work, says that he tends to "democratize" every social environment he inhabits. He likes to bring "little people" front and center, asking them how they feel and what they think, and he listens to them as if they and not the "experts" are authorities. Richard Walton, writing for the *Nation*, once nominated Terkel for the title "Common Man of the Age" for the way he has always championed the rights and opinions of those little people.[14]

Luck, says Terkel, plays a large part in his success. But "luck," as Louis Pasteur had it, "favors the prepared mind." In Terkel's case it could perhaps be called the prepared heart. He finds remarkable people to interview by knowing where to look for unremarkable people. He bumps into them on the street or on a bus; they in turn introduce him to their friends; and they all prove remarkable. Unless we believe that all people make good witnesses, we must conclude that Terkel has a special talent for discovery.

Nelson Algren once recounted the amusing story of the way Terkel, in Paris, located the mime Marcel Marceau. During his first hour there, with the first telephone call he made, on the first ring, he reached Marceau. With his minimal French he made an appointment for an interview and conducted it with impressive success. When in amazement Algren asked him if all his subjects materialized and responded that way, Terkel shrugged, "Sure, more or less."[15] This was everyday fare for him.

There are people Terkel will not interview, a few "celebrities" he shuns, first among them the supercilious William F. Buckley. Buckley annoys Terkel to a degree not readily explainable. During a lecture at Auburn University in 1990 Terkel was asked to give the keys to success. Knowing that Buckley was to speak there a month later, Terkel told his questioner to wait and ask him – then added that it helps, of course, to inherit a million dollars (Auburn). He dismisses Buckley as "a Neanderthal who speaks in polysyllabic riddles." He admits that he once agreed with a challenger that Buckley is a serious thinker but that it was 3:00 A.M. and he was drunk when he said it (*Talking*, 115).

At times Terkel's empathy and garrulity have been known to fall short. He has even on occasion flopped. On 1 January 1970, as the Nixon era was beginning to take hold of the nation, Terkel agreed to appear on the "Dick Cavett Show" if he could return to plug *Hard Times* when it appeared later that year. He was a disaster. He was in a bad mood, the audience was unresponsive to what he had on his mind, and he ended up preaching to them: "You're not the silent majority. . . . Silence is death." It was such a fiasco that Cavett's producers refused to have Terkel for the return engagement, even when *Hard Times* made the best-seller list (Koch, 87).

For some of his detractors, this incident points up Terkel's weakness as an interviewer, thus as an oral historian. They say he feels so strongly about certain social and political ideals that he lets these views color his work, his choice of subjects and witnesses, the questions he asks and thus the answers he gets, and even the way he edits his books. As an advocate of what he calls "socialism with a human face" (Galloway, 8), Terkel doubtless sees that certain points are made. Issues to him are usually black or white, seldom gray, and his "little people" do seem to confirm his ideals.

Synthesizer

Such criticism, while it must be considered, is difficult to substantiate. The original tapes of Terkel's interviews, the questions and answers that eventually appear in edited form as his oral histories, are not available for public scrutiny. We do not know in most cases the questions he asked, the tone of his voice, or to what extent he modified, rearranged, or omitted certain things. On the other hand, complete interviews, published more or less in their entirety, show Terkel to be an evenhanded interviewer.

Two such interviews, taken apparently from taped sessions, appear in the December 1972 and January 1973 issues of *Today's Health*. In both articles Terkel is moderating panel discussions: one dealing with ways to improve urban life in America and the other with the mental health of Americans. In both cases he proves to be intelligent, well informed, efficient, controlled, and considerate. He keeps the discussions moving, the participants on track, and the issues rotating fairly among the members, yet he remains unobtrusive. He gets the job done, the subjects covered, without undue interference. He does not impose his own views or debate others'. When he does make comments of his own, they are pertinent and unembellished. Even considering that the discussions were tidied up for publication, one must conclude that Terkel is a skillful and fair man with his tape recorder.[16]

In still another case, during the autumn following the nationally televised Watergate hearings, *Harper's* carried an interview arranged and conducted by Terkel with Jeb Stuart Magruder and William Sloan Coffin. Magruder, who was one of the Nixon men being accused of the cover-up behind the break-in, had said publicly that he had perhaps done the wrong thing for the right reason, that he may have violated federal law but did so for the sake of a higher law of morality, and that he had learned his "situation ethics" in Reverend Coffin's class at Williams College. Coffin had already publicly denied this last charge.

In the interview Terkel has Magruder repeat and expand on his contention that Coffin's advocacy of situation ethics and civil obedience helped explain and excuse his behavior in Watergate. He lets Coffin vigorously deny that what he taught Magruder in any way excused the cover-up, adding that if Magruder really believed what he was saying, he simply was not very bright. Although Terkel himself obviously had strong opinions about what was being said – he was a friend of Coffin and no friend of the Nixon White House – he once again demonstrates great restraint and objectivity, keeping the discussion educational, unobtrusively asking his questions without intruding on the exchange, without expressing his own opinion.[17]

An even better example of Terkel as interviewer, better because it is one-on-one, appeared in the September 1980 edition of *Saturday Review*, a conversation with playwright Arthur Miller. At that time Miller's most recent play, *The American Clock*, had just opened in New York. It depicted a middle-class family in the 1930s, hard hit by the depression, trying to survive, and Miller had noted that it was inspired by Terkel's *Hard Times*. Their conversation is more than mutual congratulation. It goes beyond conversation, beyond mere questions and answers. Terkel knows Miller's plays and can discuss them intelligently with him. He understands Miller's characters. He probes Miller's life without violating his personal space.[18]

In an interview with Jimmy Cagney for *Esquire*, a much lighter piece, Terkel demonstrates still another quality that makes him such an effective person with the microphone. At Cagney's upstate New York farm the two men talk of work and life. Terkel is informed, interested, involved, down-to-earth, moving easily from entertainment to philosophy to personal dreams and back again. He is the essential man of transition and integration, a synthesizer.[19]

Terkel has indeed raised the interview to the level of art. His interviews are in fact statements greater than the sum of their parts. His gift for synthesis was first demonstrated in 1961 when he wove together a number of voices he had collected into a radio show on celebrating life. Two of his previous shows had appeared as long-playing albums, but this one, "Born to Live: Hiroshima," proved by far the most successful – in content, form, and effect.

Terkel says he was inspired to do the show by the words of a Japanese woman describing the atomic attack on Hiroshima as well as by the words of a young man interviewed at Hull House who said,

"You are born to die, that's all." From a myriad of his collected taped interviews Terkel chose more than 30 cuts, all having to do with reasons to live, and with the help of WFMT's Jim Unrath created a collage of voices and sounds. The show first aired early in 1962, and since that time it has been played on WFMT every New Year's Day. An impressive work, it demonstrates the skill, versatility, and single-mindedness of its creator. It could just as well have been titled "Voices of Life," as it so forcefully captures and orchestrates the joyful and sorrowful sounds that compose human experience.

It begins with the voice of Myoko Harubasa, the Japanese woman who helped inspire the program, describing what it was like to be the victim of an atomic attack. She is followed by the jarringly virginal voices of a children's chorus singing the spirited song "Rise, Shine, and Give God the Glory." The boy at Hull House explains that he never worries about the future because we are born just to die, at which point Terkel asks, "Born to die? What about in between the time you're born and the time you die?" Then follow voices of life.

Two East Indian drummers compete, playing conflicting rhythms, until they realize that neither will win, then slowly reconcile and come to harmony. Art critic Alexander Eliot describes a painting by Goya, now in the Prado, in which two men engaged in mortal combat beat each other senseless before a landscape of natural beauty. Unlike the drummers, they do not see that war is useless and destructive.

Lillian Smith, the southern female novelist, describes the conflicting values she learned growing up, hearing in church the teachings of Jesus yet seeing in her society the practice of racial discrimination. When she asked about this situation, she was told that when she grew older she would understand, that to find inner peace she must simply accept the ambiguity. She found that she could not do so.

The folksingers the Weavers, featuring Pete Seeger, sing one of their numbers: "You'll weep for the rocks and mountains / When the stars begin to fall." This refrain continues to be heard through the remainder of the program. The French writer Simone de Beauvoir (an intimate of Nelson Algren) describes how she came to understand that she did not make herself, that she is a creation of her world. A "young novelist from Harlem" named James Baldwin talks about his own discovery that all of life is interconnected. Miriam

Makeba, the black South African vocalist, describes the hard life her mother lived. Georgia Tanner, a black sharecropper from Tennessee, recalls cutting wood for a living. Chicago poet Gwendolyn Brooks recites an elegy to a friend, and Terkel sighs, "Oh yeah."

Salvatore Baccaloni, an Italian operatic basso profundo, talks wistfully of a colleague who was a great singer because he was a great actor and a great actor because he became his parts. Terkel then joins the cast of Irish playwright Brendan Behan's *The Hostage* as they frolic through "There's No Place on Earth like the World," the last line disintegrating into laughter. Pete Seeger returns to admit that after all his years as a folksinger he is just learning how to tell a story. It is an art form that has almost been lost, he says, because people now sit back and let others tell their stories for them.

There follow many voices: Baldwin again, to say that he will never make peace with this world's values; Coffin, to pray for the grace to quarrel with the world; Makeba, to explain how people must have a sense of humor to survive in South Africa; a female survivor of a Nazi prison camp, to say that she is alive today because she never lost faith that she would be liberated; and, finally, a tenor, singing "The Marseillaise," a song of liberation but filled with blood.

Terkel reestablishes his theme. The Japanese woman speaks of Hiroshima, the children sing, the boy at Hull House questions life. Then there are answers: Irish playwright Sean O'Casey recites, "Be brave, be brave, and evermore be brave"; an East Indian actress tells of an old woman, herself living on the edge of starvation, who came forward during a benefit performance for Bengal relief to offer her only cow; and literary critic John Ciardi describes the voice of Caruso, the way it expands a listener's mind, demonstrating human potential.

Bertrand Russell declares that war cannot settle the great issues of world history: remember your humanity, he urges, and forget all the rest. Buckminster Fuller discusses the genius of Albert Einstein and recalls that great man's shock and despair when nuclear fission was used to make the atomic bomb. Einstein's voice comes through the years, weak and distant, yet simple and humane. The Russian writer Nicolai Pogodin speculates that Einstein may have come to us from a future time.

Arthur C. Clarke, the British science fiction writer, argues that it is not a curse, as the Chinese say, but a privilege to live in these interesting modern times. American astronomer Harlow Shapley declares that man's true enemy, his only real enemy, is himself. After echoes of previous speakers, Terkel then offers Jacob Bronowski's powerful description of his arrival in Nagasaki after the bomb fell. Coffin goes on to pray that we might leave the world with more justice, truth, and beauty than we found when we arrived. Carl Sandburg reads his verse: Man is a long time coming / Man will yet win." A mother and child sing "Happy, Happy," celebrating their love. The show ends with a thunderous choral rendition in German of "Joy, Thou Source of Light Immortal."

"Born to Live" is an impressive achievement; it won UNESCO's 1962 Prix d'Italia as the best radio documentary aimed at easing East-West tensions. In his memoirs Terkel describes in hilarious detail his trip to Verona to accept the award. It was a grand adventure: meeting famous people he had long admired, talking with common people, missing trains, arriving a day too early, sitting uncomfortably through the ritual in a rented tuxedo, accepting the award. He was presented with a scroll hand painted by a Veronese artist. On a Chicago bus a week later he took it out of its protective cylinder to have another look, forgot to replace the cap, and never saw it again (*Talking,* 147).

An American Village

Terkel could and might well have made a fine career out of producing such documentary broadcasts on topical themes. He had the skill to capture human voices and thoughts and to integrate them meaningfully. He could have moved from radio to television and even to film. Another door opened first, however, and he was so successful with this different endeavor that it commanded most of his attention from that point on: he became an oral historian.

André Schiffrin at Pantheon had heard Terkel's "Almanac" on station WRVR in New York and admired his way with musicians and writers. In 1965, having himself just been successful with Jan Myrdal's *Report from a Chinese Village*, Schiffrin approached Terkel about doing a book about an American village. Terkel at first thought it was a crazy idea. "You gotta be outa your mind," he told Schiffrin. But with persistence Schiffrin persuaded Terkel that this was something worth doing and that he was the man to do it. At last Terkel, with some misgivings, agreed to give it a try (Galloway, 9).

What American village should it be? What town was typically American? What city was interesting and varied enough to provide a complete picture of contemporary American society? What place did Terkel know well enough to find witnesses, get them to talk, and assess the value of their testimony? The answer to all these questions, after a little deliberation, was Chicago. Terkel knew Chicago and its people. Its neighborhoods were like the streets of a village, each one different, all a part of the pattern. It was typically American, with its mix of Yankees, Appalachians, blacks, Hispanics, and other ethnic groups. Chicago it would be. After all, as Terkel likes to say, "Chicago is the world" (Auburn).

Terkel may have had the audacity to choose his hometown as the American village because of Nelson Algren. In 1951 Algren had published *Chicago: City on the Make*, a book that reestablished the Windy City as a subject for serious study. He had dedicated the book to poet Carl Sandburg, who had called Chicago "City of Big Shoulders" and "Hog Butcher for the World." Terkel wrote the preface to a later edition of Algren's book, calling it the classic tribute to a great city (*Chicago*, 131).

Algren's *Chicago* is no dry treatise. Like the fiction of James T. Farrell and the poetry of Carl Sandburg, it is a creative response to a place, impressionistic, nostalgic for a time when giants roamed the earth. It captures the essence of Chicago at midcentury, at its best, at its worst. Its most memorable line – one Terkel later quoted in the preface to his own book about Chicago – says that loving Chicago is "like loving a woman with a broken nose, you may well find lovelier lovelies. But never a lovely so real."[20] For Terkel as for Algren, Chicago evokes strong and conflicting emotions. Terkel says that his feelings for Chicago have been "wildly ambivalent as far back as I can remember."

Bernard Jacobs of WFMT gave Terkel a three-month leave to do his interviews for the project. Cathy Zmuda transcribed the tapes he made to typed copy. Out of hundreds of interviews Terkel finally chose 70 and used only the distilled essence of those.[21] Becuase the book would run to 381 pages, almost all of it verbatim testimony, the amount of material Terkel accumulated must originally have been immense. He made his collection in an amazingly concentrated period of time: three months full-time, about a year total.

Terkel contended that he had no method in his search for witnesses to interview and none in interviewing them. He was armed only with his tape recorder and a hungry curiosity about the human condition – in all its Chicago variations. He had, of course, his irrepressible personality, his knowledge of the city, several hundred friends, several thousand acquaintances, several million fans, and great experience with the interview. What he had to learn as he went along was how oral history is collected. He knew little about the choice of witnesses, the objectivity, the balance, and the required validation and claimed that he cared little for such matters. Balance is particularly illusory, and not particularly important, because "we live in unbalanced times." In the preface to *Division Street*, his first oral history, he disclaimed any attempt at scholarship, especially sociology, and pointed out that the book was "neither the believer's Good News nor the doubter's bad report."[22]

He seems simply to have gone out looking for people to interview about life in contemporary Chicago, contemporary America, the contemporary world. He called what he was doing "guerilla journalism" (*Division*, xix). He had no master plan, except to search for average, normal, common people who had something to say. He purposely avoided professional writers and journalists, along with professors and clergymen, because they had other forums in which to express their opinions. He may also have reasoned that they would not give him candid commentary, accustomed as they were to expressing themselves defensively. Nor did he attempt to seek out bizarre or notorious individuals in order to make the book sensational. He did find that at times he had to overcome his own celebrity, that it inhibited conversation, but his famous ineptitude with the tape machine came to his rescue and let his subjects see that he was as common as they.

He went looking for individuals, not groups, not types. "The individual," he was convinced, "is the key to everything." He looked for the individual in his or her neighborhood, where this person actually lived. He tried to find individuals from every Chicago class, race, and faith. Some he bumped into by accident: on buses, on the street, or in bars (*Division*, xx-xxii). He followed leads, tips, hunches. Sometimes he was lucky, sometimes not. He did it all with his usual energy and zest. "To call Terkel excited," Nelson Algren said, "is a redundancy" ("Talk of the Town," 63). Chicago newspaper columnist Mike Royko claims that, while being mugged, Terkel had tried to interview his assailant as the man wrestled Terkel to the ground (Galloway, 9). With that kind of enthusiasm he was bound to write an interesting book.

Searching for some way to make people speak candidly about life in his American village, having no training for his task, and lacking the advantage of working with the kind of specified topic he would have in subsequent books, Terkel asked certain leading questions: What about the escalating war in Vietnam? What about the escalating civil rights movement at home? He found that because these were hot topics, people would first talk about them and then expand into other areas of concern. He asked about God and then about the atomic bomb but found little interest in these subjects in the mid-1960s: he concluded that these issues were simply too big for common people to handle. He was only moderately successful with one of the few questions he chose to print in the text, one that usually appears near the end of conversations: "If Jesus Christ came back today, what would happen?" Generally he got his best results when he let people ramble on about their personal concerns. What such ramblings revealed impressed the literary world.

Although Terkel oversaw this entire project and located most of his witnesses, he had an assistant do some of the interviews. He paid his subjects for their testimony. In all but 13 of the 70 cases he chose to use in the book, he gave his witnesses pseudonyms, supposedly to protect their privacy. Some told him, after the book was published and proved popular, that they wished he had used their real names. But he never regretted his decision to disguise them. He continued to do so, although to a lesser extent, in later books. Some told him how surprised they were when they saw their words in print, that they had not known they felt that way.

Terkel chose to call the book *Division Street: America*. There is a Division Street, of course, in Chicago's North Side, a major traffic artery that divides the city into distinct parts. Though Terkel crossed Division Street twice daily, he was quick to say that his title did not refer to any specific place: it was meant to be metaphor for the division in American life. He had been aware, since he was a boy listening to conversations and arguments at the Wells-Grand, of the division in this country between the haves and the have-nots. He rediscovered it in the testimony of his witnesses. The division was broader and deeper than he had expected. It went through Chicago, and it went through the nation. It epitomized modern American society. Much later he admitted, with a hint of guilt, that he has lived a good part of his life on a "have" street in a city, society, and world of have-nots (*Chicago*, 120).

Division Street: America

Terkel dedicated *Division Street: America* (1967) to the memory of three Chicagoans: the writer Ring Lardner, the architect Louis Sullivan, and Jane Addams, the founder of Hull House. These three represented the positive, creative, and humane side of his American village. In later writings he contrasted these three and their accomplishments with Al Capone and Mayor Richard Daley and theirs: the dark, destructive side of his town.

As his theme Terkel highlighted words from a speech Jane Addams gave in 1909: "We may either smother the divine fire of youth or we may feed it. We may either stand stupidly staring as it sinks into a murky fire of crime and flares into the intermittent blaze of folly or we may tend it into a lambent flame with power to make clean and bright our dingy city streets." And to emphasize the theme of Hull House's care for future generations, he began his text with the testimony of Florence Scala, who grew up near Hull House, attended classes there as a child, worked there as a volunteer, and was now trying to save old Chicago from the wreckers.

She says that she has always loved the city but that things have changed. Now she both loves and hates it. She is saddened by the decline of its neighborhoods, many of them wiped away in urban-renewal projects, so saddened that she ran (unsuccessfully) in 1964 for the city council in order to reverse the trend and now uses every opportunity to protest further destruction. She compares Chicago's urban renewal, which has just claimed Hull House, to man's biblical Fall. She is most disappointed that the people she hoped would help her – private citizens and public officials – have failed to be moved by her concern. "There's a real kind of ugliness among nice people," she muses (*Division*, 4). It is doubtful that the subsequent recon-

struction of Hull House on the campus of the University of Illinois's
Chicago branch would have changed her mind.

Terkel follows Scala with a group of people who have been
affected by the changes taking place in their city. The group appears
collectively under the title "The Feeling Tone" after a comment by
the first to speak, Lucy Jefferson: "You see, there's such a thing as a
feeling tone. One is friendly and one is hostile. And if you don't have
this, baby, you've had it" (*Division*, 18). Lucy is 52, black, up from
Mississippi, the head of a household and the mother of a son in
trouble with the law. She feels no self-pity, for the real slaves in
modern society, she contends, are white women and black men.

There is a fascinating variety among the people with the feeling
tone. Harriet Behrens, 66, a blind white woman, speaks freely about
her feelings on race but refuses to discuss religion or politics. Jan
Powers, a young professional woman, shows concern only for herself and her immediate family. The conflict in Vietnam is of concern
to her only because a younger brother may be drafted. Elizabeth
Chapin, 75, deplores the fact that all of Chicago's landmarks are disappearing. Teacher Rita Buscari, 25, is collecting signatures and
picketing to stop criminal executions. People "feel" many things.

In the section called "On the Town" Terkel contrasts two men
who represent sides of Chicago the Office of Public Relations would
just as soon overlook. Kid Pharaoh, a 37-year-old ex-prizefighter,
finding his physical skills on the decline and having no education,
has drifted into the protection racket. The anger he feels at his own
failings is beginning to be redirected toward blacks. Stan Lenard, 35,
is a homosexual whose terrible loneliness is accentuated by the way
he blames himself for desires his society tells him – and he
believes – are immoral.

In "Did You See Lord Jim?" Terkel places a third man, called
Dennis Hart, with the Kid and Stan. Dennis, who is 26, is a new
member of the ultraconservative John Birch Society. "They talk
sense," he says, pointing out that he has found no other political
group that does. Yet there is no racism in his anticommunism. He is
in fact an outspoken advocate of black rights. Terkel has found a
complex society out there.

Further contrasts come in "Two Landladies, a Cop, and the
Stranger." One of the landladies, 54-year-old Gladys Pennington,
owns a great deal of property, lives off her rents, yet finds ownership

and its responsibilities unpleasant and admits she does not keep her holdings up. Tom Kearney, who at 53 has been a Chicago policeman for 23 years, the typical Irish Catholic public servant, is so frustrated by the decline in respect for the law that he will gladly retire when eligible in two more years. This seems a pity, really, because he is an enlightened man, with an understanding of young and old, black and white, protesters and conformists. Finally there is Puerto Rican Carlos Alvarez, at 33 half his life a resident of Chicago yet still considered by many to be an alien. Although he is a city museum guard, he is brutalized by the police when off-duty.

"Nostro" is inhabited by immigrants and migrants, people who call Chicago home yet are nostalgic for the homes they left behind when they came to live in the "broken promise" land. George Drossos, 66, came from Greece in 1917. He will never return home, and, like other Chicagoans, he grieves over urban renewal. Yet he still thinks of himself as a foreigner. Billie Joe Gatewood, 19, came to Chicago from Appalachia just two years earlier, and while he loves the conveniences and luxuries of the city, he misses being able to shoot off his rifle in the woods on Saturday nights. Benny Bearskin, 45, a Winnebago Indian from Nebraska, explains that all the resident tribes in Chicago long for the lands of their ancestors and laments the way American society makes young Indians ashamed of their heritage. A Roman Catholic nun who works with domestic migrants, many of them southern Protestants, describes how she has shed her sectarianism in order to work simply as a Christian.

"Homeowner" and "Homemaker" deal with the central theme of life along Division Street: owning and keeping a home despite all of modern life's threats, real and imagined. In this section Terkel captures, in medias res, the white reaction to the civil rights movement of the 1960s. Homeowner Henry Lorenz fears blacks and argues that he owes them nothing. Hitler was not all wrong, he muses, although "he certainly fell short of right" (*Division*, 125). Mrs. James Winslow, a wealthy white Episcopalian who has tried to help blacks find housing in white Evanston, feels that the grief her activism has caused her is just part of being a modern Christian. A white blue-collar worker who invited a black colleague to his home for dinner describes the enduring bewilderment and hostility of his white colleagues and neighbors at his strange gesture of brotherhood.

Among homemakers the fears are different. Some of them fear for the safety of their children. Others worry about having no skills with which to earn a living should they be left alone. Some fear black marchers in the streets, while others fear that they have grown too old and stolid to join the marchers. Some long to be married, while others are burdened down with marital problems. Whatever the fear, it is unending.

It is at this point that readers see what Terkel is capturing. He is not after statistics – he is after real people living in a real world, and he is finding them. He warned at the outset that this was not a scholarly treatise but a slice of life. He may not have warned in sufficiently pointed language what a broad and rich slice he had discovered and was about to present.

"Noblesse Oblige" features just one person, Mrs. R. Fuqua Davies, spokeswoman for wealthy Chicagoans. Either Terkel was unable to locate others of her kind who were willing to talk with him, or he decided that after Mrs. Davies other such voices would sound redundant. The Davies have two homes, one in Lake Forest and one in the Loop, and Mrs. Davies therefore feels that she understands all sides of Chicago. She is vaguely aware that there are ugly and dangerous places out there, but she is content to be sheltered from rather than confront them. She is convinced that her city officials make the right decisions regarding safety and progress.

An "Ex-Domestic" represents the other half of Chicago, across Division Street from Mrs. Davies. Lois Arthur's testimony stands in striking contrast to that of the wealthy woman, for she lives in that ugly, dangerous part of town and believes her city is out of control, perhaps lost forever. She has no insulation from its problems and no faith in its officials. When asked what would happen if Jesus came back today, she says that he would take one look and go away again.

"Executive Suite" is inhabited by Bill Dallakamp, who bears the family name of the central characters in Terkel's play *Amazing Grace*. A corporate executive, he speaks for the Republican financial establishment as he praises the fine business climate of his city, a climate much improved by the renewal projects of Democratic Mayor Richard Daley. In complementary fashion "Celebrity" features Terence Ignatius Boyle, who knows and is known by everyone in the city, particularly those with the power to appoint people to office. Using his contacts, he has made his way up the corporate ladder to

financial security; he personifies the urban American way of con-
ducting business and sees every new problem as an opportunity to
make a deal.

Chicago has its version of Madison Avenue salesmanship, about
whose merits opinion is sharply divided. One man argues that it is
advertising that moves the city forward. Another calls admen crooks
in nice suits. Both men are in advertising. "It takes a great deal of
con to sound honest in this world," the latter jokes (*Division*, 217).
Still, he is as committed to his profession as the first man. Advertising
pays, whether you believe your copy or not.

In contrast to the admen's affluence, cynical or not, is Jesus
Lopez, "Golden Gloves." Born in Mexico, he won American citizenship by serving in the American army during World War II. He had
minor success as a prizefighter and is now a skilled laborer with a
decent wage. For him, however, the land of opportunity has been a
great disappointment; he openly admits this to himself and others,
and spends most of his days in a boozy haze.

Other "Skilled Hands" follow Lopez – some are quite young,
some older. A former black baseball barnstormer describes how he
once purposely threw games when small-town white crowds threatened his team with violence if it won. A German immigrant talks
about early attempts to organize labor unions. Whatever the story,
these people see changes coming in the field of labor and for the
most part regret it. A way of life is ending.

Then there are "Retired" witnesses. One describes the rising
cost of medical care and the terror this situation brings to the hearts
of older people. A former stockbroker whose heart condition led to
his early retirement now lives comfortably in Florida six months of
the year but returns to Chicago to haunt his old workplace. An
insurance man says he cannot wait to retire in a year, longing for the
free-and-easy life of Florida. A retired nurse fills the void in her life
by doing volunteer work for the city. A man in his eighties marvels at
all the wonderful things life still offers him.

Barry Byrne stands alone in his "Search for Delight" as the most
creative voice in the book. Despite Terkel's long association with
creative people and his extensive use of their voices in "Born to
Live," he uses them sparingly in *Division Street*. When he does, the
words have authority. Byrne, an architect who once worked with
Frank Lloyd Wright, has just returned to Chicago after an extended

absence and is able to assess the physical damage of urban revewal. Buildings, neighborhoods, people, personalities are disappearing overnight. Things will never be the same.

Four voices form the section on "The Teacher," individual voices that speak as one. Well-trained, capable, and dedicated, they face what appear to be enormous and insurmountable problems. Their schools are growing poorer and blacker, their students more hopeless and hard to manage. They sound as if they are carrying burdens too heavy for them. Once again Terkel uncovers a crisis, a powder keg ready to explode.

"Making It" features small-business men, the bedrock of the capitalist system: a saloon keeper, a grocery owner, a salesman, a buyer. They are open and articulate, yet they have little interest in the world outside their doors. Only one man, a grocer who came to Chicago from Tennessee, refuses to talk about his work, placing himself in sharp contrast to Terkel's other witnesses:

> "It's all the same to me. It don't make no difference where I'm at."
>> "Do you enjoy your work?"
>> "Yeah."
>> "Day passes by quickly?"
>> "Pretty fast."
>> "Anything gripe you?"
>> "No. (Long pause) It don't do no good to talk about it." (*Division*, 293-95)

In the end he says that when he was young he wanted to be a teacher but went into business for the money.

Terkel's "Fallaways" are people who have made significant changes in their lives. Dave Williamson sacrificed wealth and social status to work at the black West Side Ecumenical Institute. He understands the great divide between the haves and have-nots and knows the guilt that so many affluent people carry. To him Chicago is both a wonderful opportunity for humanity and a threat to mankind. Hal Malden is a former Nazi who now serves as a social worker. Arriving in Chicago from Arkansas six years earlier, reacting with fear and anger to the races and classes he had never before encountered, he became a Nazi. Now, however, he has grown, has shed his fear and anger, and approaches the new people with love and understanding.

There are two "Grass Rooters," one male and one female. Jim Campaigne, 25, has abandoned the Marxism of his college days for membership in the conservative Young Americans for Freedom. As publisher of a string of local newspapers he is trying to stem the tide of the liberal trend in American politics. By his own assessment an "easy-going" guy, he demonstrates an intensity and dedication to cause that is disturbing. Anne Grierson works in Terkel's own Uptown part of the city to establish a "Democratic society." Through the organization JOIN (Jobs or Income Now) she is trying to build a liberal "counter-society" to challenge the status quo. Soon after her conversation with Terkel JOIN's headquarters were destroyed by fire: Grierson and her fellow workers, however, planned to continue their crusade.

As he collected his interviews Terkel ran across interesting young people, and he decided to showcase eight of them in "The Inheritors." He would find places for young voices in subsequent books as well, and they often provide the keys to his various subjects. Here they tell him that their parents completely misunderstand them: they feel that the older generation is unable to express love. They speak of how hard it is to be an individual when everyone is expected to be part of a group. They talk of being on their own since childhood, of being afraid that they will not find gainful employment, and of racial prejudice. A rich boy is as detached from his society's problems as rich adults are. A poor boy is already fighting in Vietnam by the time the conversation with him is published. Terkel catches the 1960s generation in early bloom.

Having begun with Florence Scala and Hull House, having found in its demolition a theme – the sacrifice of a grand past for a sterile future – Terkel ends with Jessie Binford, who worked at Hull House from 1906 to 1963. Now 90, she lives in Iowa, and as old as she is she still empathizes with the younger generation and decries the way they are being neglected. Only a year after her conversation with Terkel she died.

Chicago and a New Career

Division Street opened a new phase of Terkel's life, gave him a new career actually, at the age of 55. It sold 26,000 copies in hardback and more than 7,000 in paper. Despite Terkel's claim that it was not a scholarly book, it was adopted as a textbook for urban sociology classes in many colleges. It was judged a veritable gold mine of information about contemporary American life. It was indeed a vivid portrait of the American population at a particularly important point in its history.

It was a labor of love: love for the city of Chicago and its people, with all their imperfections. To Terkel the "city that Billy Sunday couldn't shut down" is like good jazz music: rich, earthy, improvisational, ever-changing, switching tunes and rhythms and tones yet somehow unified. It is also theatrical, with larger-than-life heroes, villains, and comedians, more entertaining than anything to be found on the stage. It brings out the best in writers, including Terkel himself, as can be seen in his description of the Chicago snowstorm of January 1967. "The clean white snow falling, falling . . . a delightful deluge," he wrote in *Chicago*. "As though it were all at once, traffic came to a dead stop. Here and there, a lone car ever so slowly, slowly crawling along. A bus every now and then. Parked cars lovingly covered, buried for a few days under those huge white banks. And Chicago citizens making a startling discovery of their hitherto untouched selves. Strangers talked to strangers and were laughing about this strange, crazy happening. And when somebody fell down, five helped him/her up and laughed again (*Chicago*, 100-101).

Terkel has never cared much for the other large American cities. He disdains New York, the city of his birth, for its snobbishness. Los Angeles and its frenetic pace frighten him. He is an example of what has been called the second-city mentality common among Chicagoans. He is convinced – oddly enough, like his old nemesis Richard Daley – that Chicago and Chicagoans are treated unfairly by the "eastern" press, despite the fact that his books are published there and have been well treated by "eastern" critics.

Although he loves Chicago, he criticizes it as only a lover would care and have the right to do. In an article written for the *New York Times* just before the tumultuous 1968 Democratic National Convention, Terkel spoke prophetically of what was about to happen. It is fitting that this particular convention is being held in Chicago, he said, because Chicago is the epitome of the Democratic party and indeed of American politics. Chicago, which saw both Lincoln and Harding nominated by the exchange of offices for votes, is a city of political deals. Vice President Hubert Humphrey, the likely nominee, is the essential figure of such politics: adaptable, excessive, ready to cut a deal. Historic forces are about to clash, Terkel said – American values are about to collide, as they always have done in the city of Jane Addams and Al Capone.[23]

Chicago continued to be the pivot of Terkel's books, even when his "Division Street" imagery gave way to studies of the Great Depression and World War II, even when Terkel ventured outside his hometown to crisscross the nation in search of subjects. His emphasis on Chicago owed partly to convenience – it was easier to locate and interview people close by than to spend time on the road – but also partly to the fact that he continued to regard Chicago and its people as typically American. Twenty years after *Division Street* he would still be trying to capture his American village, this time under the simple title *Chicago.*

Chicago (1986) was suggested by Don Gold, who had himself done a book of interviews with elderly people called *Until the Singing Stops.* Dedicated to Terkel's bosses Norm Pellegrini and Ray Nordstrand, *Chicago* is a rambling essay of 138 pages, 53 of them photographs by five outstanding artists: Stephen Deutsch, Archie Lieberman, Marc Pokempner, Arthur Shay, and Richard Younker. Like the city itself, *Chicago* is a book of jazz, stocked with improvisational tunes and rhythms. Reviewer Stuart Dybeck called it an act of preservation, a book that captured the disparate voices of the "toddlin' town" and wove them into a majestic chorus.[24] It is the personal testimony omitted from *Division Street.*

Terkel says in *Chicago* that "Janus, the two-faced god, has both blessed and cursed" his hometown (*Chicago,* 11). The image came from Nelson Algren, but the deductions that follow are Terkel's own. Chicago is the battleground of armies that clash by day and night: the armies of Addams, Darrow, Debs, and Sullivan against those of Capone and Daley. They fight to decide whether Chicago will be a City of Man or a City of Things (*Chicago,* 13). The armies of Man would make it beautiful; the armies of Things would make it sterile. Of himself Terkel says, "Here, in Chicago, this cock-eyed wonder of a town, he is – and all of us are – twice blessed and twice deceived. And he's settled for that" (*Chicago,* 129). Janus always and in every place speaks with a forked tongue; one just has to live with it.

Chicago is a single-syllable town, Terkel says, where the buildings become simply Sears, John (Hancock), and Stan (dard Oil), demonstrating both affection and the need to hold conversations down to a minimum of words. It is, as Sandburg said, a muscular city: "Its character has been molded by the muscle rather than the word" (*Chicago*, 11). Its muscular masculinity, Terkel once told an editor, makes it hard to control, hard to tame, impossible to castrate.[25] It has big shoulders, it likes to work, and it does work, although in recent years it has become necessary to ask, "For whom?"

Though no more corrupt than other cities, Chicago is more open and colorful in its corruption. Among its citizens now there are few eagles, just a flock of hawks and a majority of sparrows (*Chicago*, 29). The leading man in Chicago's pageant of corruption, the man who wears a costume designed before the turn of the century, is Mayor Richard Daley. Terkel has never spoken well of hizzoner. In a 1968 *New York Times* article he was particularly savage. Daley is an old-time political hack, a neighborhood bully, he wrote, and easterners should not romanticize him. He may be good with Things, but with Men he is a disaster. Later that summer, at the Democratic National Convention, both liberal Democrats and the national media took aim at Daley for the way his police controlled the crowds. Terkel then had a measure of revenge on the man who razed old neighborhoods and dyed the Chicago River green on St. Patrick's Day.

Terkel's attacks on Daley, like his books on his hometown, were part of his lifelong crusade to make Chicago a better place to live. As Nelson Algren once said, "Studs Terkel took up his guardianship of the city's conscience when Sandburg laid it down." According to Algren, Terkel has persisted in interpreting the law by its spiritual rather than its legal meaning."[26] By writing and speaking about his city with such zeal, Terkel has helped both Sandburg and Algren place Chicago in a special category of American cities. In his review of *Chicago* Herbert Mitgang noted that no one has written prose poems to any other city, certainly not New York, the way Sandburg, Algren, and now Terkel have done for Chicago.[27] H. L. Mencken once said, "Find a writer who has something new and particularly American to say and says it in an unmistakably American way, and 9 times out of 10 you will find he has some sort of connection with the gargantuan abattoir by Lake Michigan."[28]

Although *Division Street* received wide attention and praise, making Terkel a literary celebrity, acclaim for the book was not universal. It left readers, as it were, divided. Norman Mark of the *Chicago Daily News* began his review of it by saying how difficult it is to find the truth about Chicago: it is like punching a pillow. Terkel had done remarkably well with his tough assignment, showing the fine art of political corruption and the tendency for banality to pass for profundity in that fair city. Mark was particularly impressed with the way Terkel had been able, without preaching, to champion the cause of society's have-nots. Terkel, he said, "can take a thing – and make it human" (Mark, 18).

Peter Lyon of the *New York Times,* however, felt that the book's greatest attraction was the way Terkel forced his readers to make judgments without attempting to make them himself. Terkel pushed no thesis, analyzed no statistics, propounded no patented solutions. Still, his witnesses were the voices of a modern morality play, demanding that judgments be made and solutions be found. This was a remarkable work, a fascinating accomplishment.[29]

Michael Schlitz, writing for the Catholic magazine *Commonweal,* welcomed *Division Street* as a book about modern people without cardboard stereotypes. Terkel had given new, fresh, complex meanings to phrases like "the voters," "the public," and "the masses." This was an "engaging, poignant, uncomfortable, and optimistic encounter with urban man: not in the living room, but in the kitchen, over beers, coffee on the stove, and dishes in the sink." It should be required reading for bishops and bureaucrats, the people who would find in its pages the very people they are supposed to be serving.[30]

There was, then, a broad consensus that Terkel had accomplished something extraordinary. Richard Stern in the *Nation* called the book a collection of portraits of people so ordinary that they are overlooked by most social research yet so important that they should be central to any social scheme.[31] Protestant theologian Martin Marty, not generally known for generous or effusive praise for new books, called *Division Street* a refreshing comment on "The Human Condition." Terkel had, against the odds, pieced together a mosaic of human life in the modern age that made sense. Instead of producing an interesting nonbook, which this might easily have become, Terkel had asked his questions, edited the answers, and written his brief introduction with such skill that he had fashioned a work of lasting significance. Marty apologized for being so kind to this new boy on the literary block.[32]

Not everyone liked *Division Street.* Although detractors' voices were generally lost in the torrent of praise, some of them raised legitimate questions about Terkel's claim to be herald of the common man. Chicago Roman Catholic priest Father Andrew Greeley, who was about to become a literary figure in his own right, wrote in the *Reporter* that while Terkel had captured "the Chicago of all of us who are caught in a love-hate relationship with that beautiful, senseless, absurd Second City," the book was marred by a strong central core of sentimentality characteristic of Chicago intellectuals, most of them either WASPs or Jews. They tend to see everything in stark black and white, good guys against bad, Greeley complained: they are the kind of purists who fail to see that Richard Daley, despite his shortcomings, has made Chicago the most efficient large city in America.[33]

The significant part of Greeley's critique is not whether Terkel and others like him did or did not like the Catholic Daley, or whether anti-Daley sentiment is to be found in the testimony of *Division Street,* but whether Terkel consciously and purposefully set out, by managing his witnesses, to prove Daley a villain. In other words, Did Terkel let his own biases affect his choice of witnesses, the way he questioned them, and the way he edited and organized their testimony? Was *Division Street* a spontaneous chorus sung by denizens of an American village, or was it an ideological treatise, indeed the ideology of puppetmaster Studs Terkel? Such questions would not go away.

Herbert Mitgang in the *Saturday Review* admired the vitality of *Division Street* but was saddened by its people's loneliness, aimlessness, and unhappiness. While he did not question Terkel's objectivity the way Greeley did, Mitgang's assessment of the book's tone implicitly raised the same issue. To what extent did Terkel choose people who he knew would say certain things in a certain tone? To what extent did he edit for the effect he got? To what extent did Terkel have a thesis to prove, an ax to grind, an ideology to expound through his witnesses? To what extent were these possible shortcomings intentional?

Mitgang's major problem with *Division Street*, however, was its formlessness. It was composed of too many bits and pieces, and he did not agree with Marty that the mosaic worked. The medium intruded on the message. As it stood *Division Street* was "excellent research in search of a book."[34] While Mitgang wondered how much Terkel had affected the testimony, he worried even more that the testimony was too loosely woven, leaving the message unclear. He thought Terkel had not included all the questions he asked, that he failed to draw conclusions about the answers he received: he should have done both things.

Explaining

Division Street made Terkel an oral historian, even if he may not have known how to be one. Notoriety came suddenly if not entirely unexpectedly, and Terkel was not quite ready for it. Not only was he a newcomer to oral history, untrained in its complexities, but the field itself was new. Terkel had wandered into it fearlessly, without tutoring, and it proved to be a playground both exhilarating and frightening.

In April 1973 the Organization of American Historians, meeting that year in Chicago and recognizing that a new form of historical research was nudging its way into the profession, set aside a place on its program to discuss oral history. Participants in this session joined Ronald Grele to interview Terkel, who by that time had produced three best-selling oral histories – *Division Street, Hard Times,* and *Working*. In turn Terkel had Grele and a panel of oral historians on his radio show, where he repeated some of what he had said at the conference and asked questions of his own. These two exchanges became chapters 1 and 2 of Grele's book *Envelopes of Sound.*

In the first chapter of *Envelopes* Terkel explains with his usual rambling clarity what he thinks oral history should be and do. The first principle to keep in mind, he says, is that fact and truth are not necessarily the same thing (Grele, 13). "Sometimes," he says, "the fact may not be literally so and yet be a truth to that person" (Grele, 57). What he values is truth, the truth of the particular person, not the fact that it may or may not match. He prefers to call his volumes "memory books" rather than oral histories because what he looks for is not historical fact but remembered truth. He tries to record individuals' personal truths, that which they believe they remember, that which helps them interpret and organize their lives. Such truths are valid whether or not they are factual. From memory emerges, higgledy-piggledy, the truth (Grele, 15).

He goes on to say that because his background is jazz music, a medium that formed his mind and style, he approached his study of the American village, the depression, and working life as a jazz musician approaches a song. He began each study with just a phrase, which became a theme, which became a tune, which became a skeleton on which to hang fully developed sounds and rhythms. He improvised, using intuition, hunches, and even chance to buttress his intellect and skill. He was careful to make sure that his witnesses were just as free to follow their own sounds and rhythms as he was himself (Grele, 12).

He admits that while he has no set method of locating his subjects, he does keep an eye open for archetypal figures, men and women who could speak effectively for an entire neighborhood or class or other stratum of society (Grele, 25). He says he looks for the common man, the kind that really makes history. Traditional historians have chronicled the thoughts and deeds of kings and scholars, but now with the tape machine it is possible and it is time to record the thoughts and deeds of people on the other end of society. This he finds to be the most exciting part of his work (Grele, 61).

He says that he simply goes about collecting interviews and lets his book grow naturally. He says he is careful not to plan his outlines too carefully or to force a book into some preconceived mold. Like Mark Twain's Huck Finn, he just heads "for the territory," the uncharted land, in search of information (Grele, 32). He likens his method to panning for gold. He stakes a claim, pans in the stream of everyday life, separates gold from silt by editing, and finally makes coins for a new book. Working with human beings, he warns, is less predictable than working with ore, yet the reward is of far greater value.

Finding people to talk with him has never been a problem; getting them to talk freely has been even less of one. "People want very much to talk," he has said; they "want to talk about their lives, those who have never been asked. If they're questioned with respect, if they feel they are listened to . . . oh, they want very much to talk."[35] The biggest task is not collecting but editing for space and clarity. "I tell the type transcriber, 'Don't leave anything out,'" he once said. "Out of a hundred pages, I might use eight. Sure, I edit it. I cut to highlight the truth, never to distort it" (McBride, 5). He never changes the words or thoughts of his witnesses, he says, although he does sometimes alter the sequence of statements.

While retaining his witnesses' grammar and syntax, he gives them anonymity. The only complaints he has received from his people come from the ones who wish he had used their real names. No one has complained of being misrepresented. The most exciting point in the whole process for him, Terkel says, is that moment when someone listens to or reads what he or she has said and learns something new about himself or herself (Grele, 40).

Finally, he makes two recommendations: (a) always maintain empathy with the person being interviewed, and (b) avoid editorial comment. The collector of people's truths must listen, understand, avoid offending, and get permission to publish what the person has said. He must be as objective as possible but remember that he is not dealing with cold statistics. While his witnesses are free to express their ideologies, the questioner must remain neutral. The result, while it cannot be perfectly balanced, should not aim to make a point (Grele, 42). Aware of the criticism that his own radical biases may have affected his books, he argues that the terms *conservative* and *liberal* are confusing and perhaps meaningless anyway. He himself might be called a conservative: one who wants to conserve the environment and the Bill of Rights.

By the early 1970s, after three best-sellers, Terkel was a commentator on the methodology of oral history. Yet he denied, correctly it seems, that he himself was an oral historian. Some of his books were oral history, some were not, some were mixed. He was more an entertainer than a scholar, yet through his entertainment he enlightened. His objectivity was still questioned, but not his art – or the value of his work.

Chapter Three

Suffering, Working, and Talking

The historian must be able both to recover and to recount the past for the present and the future. To "do" history requires both research (finding, sifting, judging) and narration (organizing, writing, revising). Research and narration must then be equal partners. The historian whose narration surpasses his research tends to sophism; the historian whose research surpasses his narration tends to tedium. Studs Terkel is neither a sophist nor a bore.

Opinion on the value of history is mixed. While Arthur Schopenhauer declared it virtually worthless because "Clio, the muse of history, is as thoroughly infected with lies as a street whore with syphilis," David Hume considered it to be of the highest worth as a means of "discovering the constant and universal principles of human nature." Terkel believes, as he explained to Ronald Grele's oral history group and has said in numerous essays, that he avoids the usual lies of historical narrative by disclaiming any attempt to find hard facts.[1] He searches only for memories, for the personal truths of his witnesses. He believes he uncovers the constant and universal principles of human nature, but only by giving voice to the memories, the personal truths, of the common man.

By Word of Mouth

Oral history tries to avoid some but not all of the controversy over traditional history's method and worth by dealing with events still lying within the memory of living witnesses. It may compare its oral testimony with written records – diaries, letters, recorded comments – but it does not deal primarily with accounts written by persons who may now be dead. Yet while it avoids some of traditional history's pitfalls, it follows a pathway beset by many of its own. In the

words of Robert Louis Stevenson, "The obscurist epoch is today."
The present is too near for objective judgment, and it is impossible
to find witnesses whose memories are not affected by subsequent
events, however recent the period under scrutiny. It is, then, essential to treat oral testimony as critically as traditional historians have
treated written records, perhaps more so.

On the other hand, historians of various persuasions generally
agree that oral history, the testimony of eyewitnesses, is of great
value. John Ruskin once said that the only history worth reading is
"what was done and seen, heard out of the mouths of the men who
did and saw," and Giovanni Battistia Vico agreed: "History cannot be
more certain than when he who creates the things also narrates
them." Henry David Thoreau put it this way: "Where a battle has
been fought, you will find nothing but the bones of men and beasts;
where a battle is being fought, there are hearts beating." Oral history, whatever its limitations, captures the words that flow from such
battles.

Oral testimony has played a part in the writing of history from
the earliest Greek experiments with the art form. In writing of the
Persian Wars Herodotus used the memories of men, some quite old,
who had participated in those battles. His successor Thucydides was
himself a participant in the Peloponnesian War that he chronicled
using the testimony of his comrades. Yet when history as a science
was revived in the early modern age and came to maturity in the
nineteenth century, practitioners of this science tended both to write
about ages so far removed as to have no living eyewitnesses and to
have more regard for letters and journals than for the tranquil
recollections of old men and women.

The resuscitated science of history emphasized the worth of
documents from the past, critically compared, over the subjective
memories of "those who were there." Thus history was based on the
witness of the literate and the articulate, not on the words of the
often-illiterate commoner. History in its "legitimate" form was elitist.
Oddly enough, oral history, in its earliest modern forms, was so as
well.

What came to be known as oral history was formalized in this
country during the New Deal, as part of the WPA's Federal Writers'
Project. One of the federally funded proj-ects was for writers to
interview needy families, and the testimonies of these common

people were often recorded verbatim and preserved, regardless of whether they could be verified for accuracy. From this project came the first tentative steps, the first methodology, the first practitioners of a new art. While Terkel has not attributed his own inspiration or method to this project, he knew of it. He did surveys himself, and the effort to capture the memories and opinions of common people doubtless had an impact on his imagination.

The officially recognized birthplace of systematic oral history was the Oral History Project begun in 1948 at New York's Columbia University. It was by definition an elitist undertaking – to "debrief" "the Great Men" before they passed on – and was concerned primarily with political and diplomatic history.[2] The person most closely associated with its birth was Allan Nevins, although he disclaimed credit for it. The person most closely associated with its development, the man who directed the project for 24 years, was Louis Starr. Earlier and perhaps more descriptive phrases, such as "oral documentation" and "living history," eventually gave way to the more direct, more easily remembered, but probably less accurate "oral history," coined by Joe Gould. While some critics argued that the phrase was misleading, it won the day, and still claims the title.

Most traditionalist historians were at first unwilling to acknowledge oral history as a valid branch of the profession. Few of them practiced it, except in its most elitist form and then only to buttress more traditional methods, leaving its cultivation to a few renegades and to amateurs like Terkel. Only slowly and in fits and starts did it gain credibility and acceptance. It did so (and for a time in the 1970s even became faddish) by developing its own rules of verification, admitting and living within its natural limitations, and joining the broader field of historical research as a cooperative tool of the science.

Its progress toward acceptance was aided by a distinction made by its practitioners between oral history and oral tradition. The latter was said to be information passed down from person to person, generation to generation, through many ages, transitions, and reinterpretations. Oral history, by contrast, had to be testimony from a person present at the time and place of an event under examination; furthermore, oral history had to acknowledge that, given the weaknesses of human memory, the human tendency to filter and interpret events to suit present needs, it would always be a limited science.

Such distinctions and limitations having been made and admitted, oral history came in from the cold and became a member of the history household, settling down, warts and all, to a place at the family table. By the late 1980s the Oral History Association had published a complete set of "Evaluation Guidelines" for its practitioners to follow.[3]

Oral history as now accepted by the profession can boast many advantages of information gained by word of mouth. The testimony of eyewitnesses provides information often not found in written documents, public or personal. It captures the memories of nonelitist, nonliterate, previously inarticulate witnesses. By asking direct questions of living witnesses, it can provoke responses that even literate and articulate witnesses might otherwise neglect to record. It can capture the personalities, often quite complex, of its witnesses as written records might not do. Because it permits the historian to ask follow-up questions, it can make clarifications and add depth and dimension to what might otherwise be confusing, superficial, or narrow testimony.

There are, of course, methodological problems inherent in the very nature of oral history. Interviewers might be unskilled or possess debilitating biases, and such matters may be difficult for readers and listeners to recognize. Questions asked of witnesses can be slanted, facial expressions and body language prejudicial, and editing ideological. A sampling can be unrepresentative of the potential pool of witnesses, either because the researcher is lazy or because he chooses people who will help him make a point. He or she can misinterpret, accidentally or purposefully, the testimony gathered.[4]

Michael Frisch, in his enlightening book *A Shared Authority*, suggests ways to limit such abuses and to make oral history a more valuable, less risky enterprise. He specifically suggests that readers ask three questions about whatever testimony they find: (a) What sort of person is speaking? (b) What sort of subject is the person talking about? and (c) What sort of statements is the person making about the subject? While asking such questions cannot correct all the faults of all oral historians, doing so can keep the testimony itself in perspective.

Of all Terkel's books only two are self-proclaimed oral histories: *Hard Times* and *"The Good War." Division Street, Working, American Dreams, The Great Divide*, and *Race* do not address specific historical periods or events. They are, however, oral testimony – about people's lives, their working and living conditions, their hopes and dreams – the stuff of oral history, available for use by future historians. Terkel has produced seven (eight, if we count the autobiographical *Talking to Myself*) of the most widely read and discussed books of oral testimony, if not always pure oral history, in the modern age. His books demonstrate all the advantages and disadvantages, the strengths and weaknesses, the rewards and dangers, of oral studies.

Terkel has uncovered previously unknown facts, captured heretofore-unknown personalities, filled gaps, added color and clarity to past events, added to public knowledge the testimony of persons unlikely ever to have made contributions to historical understanding without him. On the other hand, readers must keep in mind that his witnesses are interpreting their memories after years of intervening experience, that their memories are at best faulty and at worst untruthful, that they tend to conceal painful or unattractive memories, that they will repeat hearsay as fact, and that their perspectives are often one-dimensional. Owing to space limitations Terkel often abbreviates and probably oversimplifies his witnesses' testimony. And owing to his own assumptions, biases, and inadvertant misinterpretations, he can control, prejudice, and even misrepresent the testimony.

In Terkel the strengths and weaknesses of the oral historian are exaggerated. He is a superior scout for witnesses and a most effective questioner. He knows how and where to find subjects and how to evoke responses from them that ring true and are full of surprises. He fills his pages with color and humanity. Yet he has no systematic method of choosing his witnesses and no desire for balance. He pays his witnesses for their time. He does not show what questions he asks, and no one knows to what extent his body language and facial expressions direct people to act and speak as they do. He refuses to weigh, evaluate, or draw conclusions about the testimony he finds. To use the gold-mining metaphor that Terkel finds so pleasing, he is a superb prospector, an excellent panner, but a questionable minter of coins.

He is honest and forthright about his disregard, disdain even, for historical fact. It matters little to him whether the memories of his people match the events described in history books. He would doubtless agree with Frederic Maitland, who once said, "The essential matter of history is not what happened but what people thought or said about it." Terkel knows that, in the final analysis, he is not "doing" oral history but is rather recording people's memories of history. The professional oral historian prints the questions he or she asks and the conclusions drawn from the responses. The oral historian places the testimony in context and compares it with established historical fact. Indeed, Christopher Lehmann-Haupt says that by failing to include his questions, by editing for space, and by refusing to draw conclusions, Terkel destroys the oral history he so effectively collects.[5]

Despite the misgivings of many critics, however, most other oral historians applaud Terkel's work. There has appeared in print little of the jealous sniping one might expect when an amateur in a certain field scoops the professionals and makes off with the big bucks. Most oral historians admire the work Terkel does and credit him with helping popularize their field, providing them with an audience they would not otherwise have.

Samuel Hand, for instance, excuses Terkel's loose methodology, his lack of objectivity, and his refusal to admit his biases or draw his conclusions – all of which he might criticize in a fellow professional oral historian – by calling him a "freelance."[6] What makes Terkel so valuable, Hand says, is that while he is a pop writer, he shares with his more archivist colleagues the view that events are significant because they affect the lives of ordinary people. Gary Okihiro compares Terkel with such writers as Arthur Schlesinger, Jan Vansina, and Staughton Lynd, saying that they all share two convictions: (a) that the recorder of history must shed the intellectual arrogance that presumes to know more than those who offer testimony about great events and (b) that nonliterate (better, nonliterary) people have no feeling for what is historically significant.[7] Professional oral historians accept Terkel not because he is always professional but because his presumptions and instincts are essentially sound.[8]

Hard Times

Late in the 1960s, again at the urging of André Schiffrin, Terkel began collecting interviews for a second Pantheon book. He was looking for memories of the Great Depression, a period he considered the turning point of his own life. Times were hard then, "but we were alive," he once told me. Unlike *Division Street*, which was about contemporary Chicago, the new book was about a time past, an oral history more than just oral testimony. *Hard Times* was published in 1970, its title coming from one of the witnesses, a man who had come from Appalachia and landed in Chicago in the 1930s, when he was 14: "I never heard that word 'depression' before," he told Terkel. "They would all just say 'hard times' to me. It still is."

Division Street had not been called oral history, but *Hard Times* bore the subtitle "An Oral History of the Great Depression." The earlier book had appeared before the phrase "oral history" was commonly used to sell books. Now it was known – as the catch-phrase for a growing literary movement – and Terkel or Schiffrin decided to take advantage of it. In this book Terkel identified his speakers more fully and even used many of their real names. While he still did not indicate all the questions he asked, he included more of them than he had done in *Division Street*. Still, he preferred to stand aside, at least on the printed page, and let his speakers take center stage.

Hard Times is a greater book than *Division Street*: better focused, better organized, broader in human and geographic scope, a heaping bowlful (529 pages) of memories. *Division Street* is a grand collection of personal opinions and folk histories, and while it offers a wide portrait of modern men and women and made universal statements about modern American urban life, it is limited to one year in one city. *Hard Times* offers the story of an entire nation passing through perhaps its most trying time.

It is dedicated "For my wife, my son and my editor," and Terkel takes pains to thank Cathy Zmuda, who transcribed the tapes, and his colleagues at WFMT, Norm Pelligrini, Ray Nordstrand, and Lois Baum, who aided and encouraged him through the two years of interviewing and editing. Once again he gives little interpretation. What he does say on the depression is of a personal nature, limited to seven pages at the start of the book.

"This is a memory book," he begins, "rather than one of hard fact and precise statistic." Aware of the criticism leveled at *Division Street*, he says that he did not search for dates and facts but went out "to get the story of the holocaust known as the Great Depression from an improvised battalion of survivors" (*Hard Times*, 3). In the introduction to a collection of excerpts from *Hard Times* that appeared in *American Heritage*, Terkel further excuses the absence of statistical analysis and analytical interpretation by saying that he was aiming for a higher goal: the memories and emotions of eyewitnesses some three decades after the event.[9]

Memories and emotions he did capture, a wealth of them. Book 1 opens with three accounts of the famous "Bonus March" on Washington in June 1932. As soldiers led by Douglas MacArthur attacked and dispersed American World War I veterans demanding their bonuses, the inadequacies of the old Hoover regime became painfully apparent, as did the necessity for a change in government. It was at this time that Yip Harburg composed the song that responded to the marchers' desperation and set the theme of hard times, "Brother, Can You Spare a Dime?"

Under "Sgt. Pepper's Lonely Hearts Club Band," the title of a Beatles tune from the 1960s, Terkel features the comments of people too young to remember the depression, those who know it only through the memories and habits of their parents, those for whom Terkel prepared the book. The younger generation says that the depression was what made the older one so greedy and unloving. One of the speakers, apparently in part because of parental treatment, committed suicide soon after his interview with Terkel. It was in collecting this series of stories that Terkel found his thesis of the direct link between the economic chaos of the 1930s and the generation gap of the 1960s. He found enough blame to go around. Introducing the segments of *Hard Times* excerpted in the *Atlantic*, he writes of this younger generation who, despite certain attractive qualities, "live today amid affluence that, to put it stuffily, makes them a deprived generation – deprived of the sometimes valuable experience of deprivation."[10]

There follows the testimony of people who knew this deprivation: those forced by hard times onto the road. In "Hard Travelin'" come the stories of hobos and of sedentary people who watched them pass. Poverty and the road tended to break down artificial social barriers, even racial ones, during the depression, for the road created an army of have-nots, men and women without property, without social status, and thus without class distinctions. The only exception seems to have been the wall between Anglos and Hispanics, which apparently never yielded, perhaps because of language, perhaps because of religion.

People of property, watching the army of have-nots roaming their countryside, were afraid and thus unsympathetic. Soup lines both saved and shamed the homeless: saved bodies, shamed souls. Cesar Chavez, at the time he talked with Terkel president of the United Farm Workers of America union, describes in moving detail how his own family, after years of farming their own land, were forced to hit the road, to pick crops for others. At the time the only hope offered the homeless lay in New Deal programs and the development of labor unions.

In "The Big Money" Terkel shows what it was like to be rich in a time of poverty. Those who knew how to use hard times, to market products that people continued to buy despite their financial woes, did not suffer at all. Nor did those with skills needed by moneyed interests. The Great Depression in fact widened the existing economic division in American society, between those who could, for example, afford psychiatrists and those who simply had to cure themselves or go insane. Throughout the book it is not hard to distinguish between people on the two sides of the divide by listening to what each one says about Franklin Delano Roosevelt and his New Deal programs for the poor.

In "Man and Boy" a 68-year-old black man tells Terkel that the depression was easier on the black man than on the white. The black man, he explains, had been poor all along and did not feel so much a failure when he brought only a bag of beans home to his woman at night. The white man, accustomed to bringing home steaks, was humiliated when all he had were beans. White women, he noted, constantly reminded their men of their failings and pressed home the humiliation.

"God Bless the Child" features adults who experienced hard times as children. They speak of being cold, hungry, even destitute. Electricity went off because bills were not paid. Families found it necessary to move from houses to garages. Parents who could not live with the terrible reality of life in hard times tried to deny the truth, left home, or died young. Children went to orphans' homes, where they talked of better times and wondered what had happened to them. Fathers are the tragic heroes of most memories: men who had once been proud breadwinners, now reduced to penury and shame, either sitting in a stupor or stirring themselves to join labor unions in order to fight the hard times.

In "Bonnie Laboring Boy" and "Three Strikes" Terkel captures the excitement of organizing to bargain collectively. America was for a time close to revolution, from both the Right and the Left, and only some mysterious faith in the system kept it from happening. Young workingmen of the 1970s, the workingmen of the 1930s say, do not know what the old guys had to suffer to give them the way of life they now lead. Three strikes are remembered: the 1936 United Automobile Workers (UAW) sit-down strike at the General Motors plant in Flint, Michigan; the Memorial Day 1937 Republic Steel of Chicago strike; and the 1940 UAW strike at Ford in Detroit. These stories show that workingmen were ready, driven by desperation, to run risks to improve their lot; that management was determined to resist collective bargaining with any force required; and that today's young workers indeed have no idea of what their accorded privileges have cost the older generation.

Book 2 details the way the depression affected professional people and their families. Being a member of one of the "Old Families" was an American profession in and of itself. Having before 1930 felt obligated to set a moral example for the lower classes, such people tried desperately to keep up their act, even when they no longer had the money to do so. Some of them pretended that nothing had changed; some left comfortable nests to become social workers; and some even became radical reformers. Many of the old families that survived the depression did so mostly on pride and tradition.

A "Member of the Chorus," Terkel's old balladeer buddy Win Stracke, spins a delightful if somewhat tragic tale of being fired from a church choir because he also sang at labor rallies. Ironically, the very man who spoke for the church when it dismissed him was himself loaning money at interest to union organizers. Win concludes that apparently "It's all right to loan money to strikers at interest, but don't sing for 'em for nothing" (*Hard Times*, 187).

"High Life" is about hard times entertainers: Sally Rand, the fan dancer; a restaurant owner who rose during the depression from waiting on tables to being boss; a composer who went around with $1,000 bills in his pockets; a six-day bicycle racer; a barnstorming boxer with connections to the mob; and the artist son of a rich father who could indulge his passion for photography while others starved.

These people, with skills to sell, with services other people were willing to pay for, with family money, recall the depression with amusement. For them it had not been so bad.

In a brief, poignant story "At the Clinic" a psychiatrist tells of studies he made among the poor in the spare time he spent away from his wealthy patients. He found that men were hurt more by the way their wives treated them than by hard times themselves. He also found that these men tended to blame not the economy, not the wealthy, not the government, but themselves for the problems they brought home to their angry women. This sense of personal responsibility for the intolerable conditions, this strange form of American individualism, helps to explain why the nation did not face the Communist or fascist revolutions other nations experienced.

"Sixteen Ton" describes the tribulations of coal miners: low wages, crippling work, dangerous working conditions, disasters, silicosis, alcoholism, strikebreakers, the necessity of leaving home and family to find better work, the expatriate mentality of Appalachians living in northern cities 30 years after the move. "The Farmer Is the Man" complements the picture by describing the perils of agricultural life: foreclosures, having to burn farm products in order to raise prices, protest marches on state capitols, violence against persons held responsible for low prices, natural disasters, and, finally, a world war that saved some farmers only to destroy many more.

Book 3 finds Terkel moving farther afield, outside his hometown, outside the Midwest and Upper South, and here his witnesses are well known. In "Concerning the New Deal" he captures the various political, economic, and personal comments of Raymond Moley, who argues that FDR alienated him by moving abruptly to the left in 1935; of James A. Farley, the political adviser whose only complaint against FDR was the way he treated all his assistants with patrician condescension; and of Burton K. Wheeler, who could have been FDR's vice-presidential running mate in 1940 had he been able to trust the man's liberalism. Then featured by himself in "An Unreconstructed Populist" is Congressman Wright Patman of Texas, a hero to bonus marchers and a villain to big business, who thinks FDR and his programs were too cautious. While talking with Terkel in 1969 Patman happens to say that from his own modest apartment he can see the Watergate Inn, "where the Cabinet lives." Three years later a break-in there brought to light the kind of corruption in high places Patman spent his career fighting.

In sharp contrast to Patman's memories is the "Peroration" of Hamilton Fish, the former congressman from upstate New York who in 1969 was still convinced that the HUAC had saved American society from communism. Roosevelt, he argues with his old zeal, sold the nation into socialist bondage, then into world war, just to get himself elected again and again. Only a few firm hands working for the Right kept him from bringing the nation to total collapse. If Patman is the unreconstructed populist, Fish is the unreconstructed reactionary. Neither man seems to have changed one bit since hard times.

In "The Doctor, Huey, and Mr. Smith" personal acquaintances recall three radical depression-era leaders: the rural physician Francis Townsend and his plan to help the aged poor; Governor and then Senator Huey P. Long of Louisiana, with his program of Share Our Wealth, which led to nationwide acclaim and assassination; and radio-orator-cum-fascist-leader Gerald L. K. Smith. The alternate voices to FDR's New Deal liberalism were ambitious, articulate, and violent.

"The Circuit Rider" is southern evangelist Claude Williams, who began his preaching career as a socially unconcerned fundamentalist but after experiencing hard times became a spokesman for the South's laboring poor. He enjoys recalling how he was "run out of the best communities, fired from the best churches and flogged by the best citizens" in Dixie for his outspoken defense of the social gospel. He is a radicalized Bible thumper who one day woke up to realize that the "Good News is only good when it feeds the poor." He and others like him helped make social concern a threat to the establishment by girding it with religious zeal and proclaiming it in religious terminology.

Historian Christopher Lasch tries in "A View from the Woods" to put the New Deal in perspective. The programs and system effected by the Roosevelt administration were inevitable, and had they been pushed to their logical conclusions they would have produced a better social system than we have today. His testimony is supported by two men whose fathers survived hard times: one who says his old man uses the fear of another depression as an excuse for piling up more and more money; the other who wonders how his father can still believe in the oxymoronic phrase "welfare capitalism."

Three people recall "Campus Life" during hard times. Every imaginable ideological movement fought for attention and converts on the nation's campuses. Students suffered physical breakdowns from malnutrition but plugged valiantly on, determined to get that college degree, the key to success and security. Clashes between radical students and reactionary deans led to suppression and in turn further rebellion. One former student radical, by 1970 a Wall Street financier who can only watch contemporary campus demonstrations on television, says with a sigh, "I was a troublemaker then. (Laughs) I wish I still were" (*Hard Times*, 397).

Book 4 is a bit of a hodgepodge of memories that do not quite fit together, do not fit anyplace else, yet are too important to be discarded. Among the interviewees are a bookmaker whose work never lagged during hard times; a man who, being in prison from 1919 to 1950, knew that good times had turned to hard times and then to wartime by the kind of food he got during each period, who feels that in general he was better off inside during the hard times than out; and movie star Myrna Loy, who can think only of all the prominent politicians who, during hard times, fell over one another to flatter her.

Book 5, by contrast, contains some of the most powerful testimony of the entire book, all of it told in the most articulate manner. Practitioners of "The Fine and Lively Arts" discuss the Federal Theater Program, the Artists' Union, and the wonders of traveling through depression America as entertainers. The various and sundry kinds of artists were just as hungry as other laborers during hard times, but the kind of creative work they did seems to have kept them alive and given them comfort. Two of the witnesses, however, did not suffer at all. They had successful Broadway plays and saw poverty only through railway-car windows.

In "Humor and Humiliation" Terkel's wife, Ida, speaking as the social worker "Eileen Barth," recalls the humiliation of that unemployed railroad man who had to let her look through his closets. Others describe their embarrassment at standing in soup lines – proud, independent people now looking to government programs or private charity for life and health. Yet there is evidence that from their deteriorating social condition such people drew strength. While the older generation learned to survive hard times, the younger learned to overcome them. In "Strive and Succeed" they tell how they used adversity to make themselves strong. Also, theirs were the children of the 1960s, who rebelled against what they considered their parents' materialistic greed.

Hard Times ends with an epilogue by a young man and an elderly woman. Nineteen-year-old Reed comes from an upper-middle-class home. When he confided to his father, whose life was molded by the depression, that he wanted to take a raft down the Mississippi River, his father suddenly opened up to him and told him how he had never been able to live out the dreams of his own youth. "It wasn't as if it was a memory, but an open wound," the boy muses. "He talked about the Depression as if it had just happened yesterday. We touched a nerve" (*Hard Times*, 527). Virginia Durr, from an aristocratic Alabama family, recalls the suffering she saw during hard times, the way people blamed themselves for their misfortune, how it changed her private and public philosophy forever. "Oh no, the Depression was not a romantic time," she says (*Hard Times*, 527). Out of it came the two kinds of adults recognizable a generation later: (a) those out to accumulate wealth as a hedge against the possible return of hard times and (b) those out to change a system in which hard times will inevitably return.

The Critics

Hard Times received more critical attention than had *Division Street*. Reviews appeared in a wide range of periodicals, from popular to scholarly. For the most part they were quite favorable. The general opinion was that Terkel had done it again – and even better this time. Excerpts appeared in *American Heritage, Atlantic,* and the *New York Times,* adding to interest, giving the book more visibility, boosting sales, and leading to even more reviews than might otherwise have appeared.

Henry Resnick in the *Saturday Review* credited Terkel with popularizing if not actually inventing a new literary genre, one born of the tape recorder's seemingly endless potential.[11] Richard Rhodes in the *New York Times* called *Hard Times* a book of startling epiphanies. He was surprised to learn that people blamed themselves for their woes, that white women were harder than black ones on their failed men. He was impressed by the "extraordinary depths of the memories Mr. Terkel evokes." Terkel had made his witnesses forget about the machine that was recording their pain, joy, shame, humor, and irony. He had laid out their souls for us to make our own judgments. This was a modern Domesday Book or St. Peter's Ledger. It put fictional accounts of the depression to shame.[12]

In his review for the *New Yorker* L. E. Sissman wrote, "Unless my ear has failed me, there is no other record as full and as faithful of the American voices of the time before our time." He too was impressed with the discoveries Terkel had made, particularly those concerning the depression's effects on subsequent American history. He was intrigued by Terkel's thesis that hard times had created three generations: the first overly prudent, the second overly acquisitive, and the third overly protected, without memory of economic hardship and frightfully ill-equipped to deal with it if and when it should come again.[13]

Terkel's friend Nelson Algren, reviewing for the *Nation*, agreed with Sissman that his generational development was the most significant of Terkel's many discoveries. The younger generation had grown up watching their parents busily storing up nuts for the winter they expected to come, and out of contempt for all this, perhaps because the storing had come at the expense of showing them love, they had decided to throw it all away. Wrote Algren, "The Great Depression put the dusty taste of early failure on the tongues of the fathers. A war economy dissolved the depression but not that taste. They wheeled, still young, through the forties and fifties: and wheeled so furiously it was hard to tell whether they were in pursuit or flight."[14]

Algren's review would in fact have made a wonderful (and muchneeded) final chapter for *Hard Times*. "The parents' dread of economic risk engendered a kindred fear of emotional risk: it was safer, more consoling, to express love through gifts of money value than through personal expression," he wrote with amazing clarity. This was the part of their parents' ethic that young people were in the process of rejecting. Whether Terkel fully recognized just what he had discovered before Algren and others pointed it out to him is unknown. He did, however, make it a theme and thesis of his later work.

Among the reviews there appeared a few cautious warnings and a number of tentative questions. Geoffrey Wolff of *Newsweek* expressed the hope that *Hard Times* would not – as he anticipated – become merely a museum of American speech. He saw it as raw material for further study, an interim rather than a finished work. If the words Terkel had coaxed out of his eyewitnesses were left alone, if they were not analyzed and made part of a larger study, they would represent wasted effort.[15]

In his review Nelson Algren saw an even greater dilemma. Terkel had kept the speeches brief, in order to include as many as possible, and this made the book seem shallow. As a friend Algren hastened to say that Terkel's great sensitivity, his bedside manner so to speak, had brought forth enough brief, intimate revelations to cover his subject adequately. Still, Algren admitted that the brevity of the stories, the wide range of their subject matter, and the great numbers of witnesses did open the door to charges of superficiality.

Saul Maloff, writing for *Commonweal*, believed that *Hard Times* needed closer, more critical editing. There were too many witnesses, their speeches were too diverse and unconnected, and the book as a whole lacked unity and cohesion. In a number of places it was slack, adrift, confusing. There was plenty of gold here, to be sure, but there was also too much dross. What *Hard Times* needed was a critical editor with a sharp pencil.[16] Maloff's point was made when Terkel prepared excerpts of the book for various magazines: editing for space, he presented only a few speakers, organized them into a tighter thematic pattern, and produced pageants that proved more effective than the book.

Christopher Lehmann-Haupt, writing for the *New York Times*, raised another question. Could a printed book of typed transcripts, edited down by more than 75 percent, in fact be an oral history? *Hard Times* had no faces, gestures, or voice tones. Speeches were abbreviated and modified by editing. Answers came without the questions that prompted them. He implied that only Terkel's original tapes were true oral history, that perhaps only videotapes were the real thing, and that perhaps the idea of oral history was itself fanciful. Whatever it was or was not, *Hard Times* seemed to him good browsing but poor reading (Lehmann-Haupt, 39). He was the first but not the last to suggest that Terkel was more discussed than read.

Bernard Weisberger went even further. *Hard Times*, he wrote in the *Washington Post Book World*, was not really history, oral or otherwise. It was merely a loose grouping of memories about a time past, with little organization and even less cohesion. He admitted that it was full of sudden insights and memorable phrases but argued that it suffered from a "formlessness that stems from the work's very nature." He called it, as Algren could not bring himself to do, a nonbook. It was "the uncut script of a T.V. or radio documentary show."[17] For him Terkel's training as a mass-media entertainer was showing through his literary guise.

Despite the words of faint praise and the questions raised by critics, *Hard Times* sold well: 62,000 copies in hardcover and 34,000 more in a paperback edition issued in 1986. It also sold well in English-speaking countries abroad, particularly in Britain, where the *Times* of London called it a significant achievement and contribution to the field of oral history. The *Times* reviewer was impressed by the discovery that unlike Europeans, who tended to blame "the powers that be" for their hard times, Americans blamed themselves. He also hinted at the ever-widening gap between the languages spoken in Britain and in America by suggesting that the British edition could have used a glossary of Americanisms.[18]

Hard Times proved to be one of Terkel's most influential works. Widely read (or at least scanned) and discussed (even if superficially), it helped to popularize oral history and consequently to make Terkel an important literary figure. The recorded voices of witnesses later comprised a two-record set, from which a stage play was derived. Arthur Miller credited the book with inspiring his 1981 play *The American Clock,* a series of vignettes in which 10 men and 5 women tell, in song, their individual stories of hard times.

Working

As soon as *Hard Times* was published and showed signs of being a success, Terkel agreed with Pantheon's Schiffrin that his next oral history would deal with the subject of work. While he gave Schiffrin credit for coming up with the idea, it was doubtless his study of hard times that helped Terkel see how important working is to Americans: how they seek it so diligently, miss it so badly when it is gone, and measure themselves and their worth by it. Again Terkel spent more than a year interviewing and another year organizing and editing the material. The finished product, *Working,* appeared in 1974.

While Terkel's titles got briefer, his subtitles got longer. To *Working* he added the explanation "People Talk about What They

Do All Day and How They Feel about What They Do." But the book would always be known simply as *Working*. He could have titled it "Labor," although this would have given it political and ideological shadings he did not want it to have. Using the Anglo-Saxon rather than the Latin term gave it the earthy quality he did want. Using the gerund rather than the noun form *work* gave it the active quality he wanted as well.

The dedication is cryptic: "For Jude Fawley; for Ida, who shares his vision; for Annie, who didn't." When I asked him what it meant, Terkel explained that his wife, Ida, shared the vision of Thomas Hardy's title character in *Jude the Obscure*, while his mother, Annie, did not. He mentions 28 "scouts" who helped him locate and interview his witnesses, among them news commentator Bill Moyers and Ida Terkel. He lists as "associates" Myriam Portnoy and Dian Smith, who helped do the interviews. Cathy Zmuda once again transcribed the tapes, while Nellie Gifford helped trim the great mass of material down to size.

Trimming was certainly needed. Terkel books were growing longer. *Division Street* had introduced 70 subjects in 381 pages. *Hard Times* had jumped to 166 witnesses in 529 pages. While *Working* dropped to 134 speakers, it rose to 589 pages. Even at that, Terkel says, it was strenuously edited. In its original bulk it was gargantuan. Again Terkel chose to print few of his lead or follow-up questions and to confine his few interpretations and comments to a brief introduction. He did provide a bit more atmosphere, fuller settings for some of the interviews, more biographical information on some of his witnesses, and postscripts to indicate what happened to some of them after the interviews. Still, this book, like its predecessors, is primarily a book of voices.

Working proved to be Terkel's most controversial book, when it was first published and even long afterward. The controversy owed in part to the book's language: whereas earlier books had contained profanity – references to God and to where one might go after death, the occasional mild curse – *Working* let witnesses refer to bodily functions of various sorts. Its street English, which some people considered obscene, caused offense.

A more widespread and critically important reason for the book's notoriety, however, was its vivid portrait of working people. Americans were supposed to love their work, to be elevated by it, to be less than themselves without it. It was as a proud boast that Mayor Daley called Terkel's own Chicago "The City That Works." Work was believed to be ennobling and fulfilling. The story that Terkel let his witnesses tell – this time not about the past but about the here-and-now – was quite a different tale.

While being out of work could indeed be frustrating and financially devastating, while being told one was unqualified for work could be humiliating, most of Terkel's people made it clear that they worked only to make a living. They took little pride or pleasure in their work, and those who worked hardest called it a form of slavery. For most Americans working was monotonous, dangerous, or degrading.

Tremendous energy, resilience, dedication, humor, and fortitude are present in these stories. Some of the vigorous complaints the stories articulate can be put down to the fact that Americans like to complain, particularly about their work, which is often the core of their lives. There is little talk here of quitting or moving on, although it must be said that quitting is a luxury reserved for the rich and moving for the skilled. For most of the witnesses, as expected, work is indeed the way they define themselves. Yet the underlying tone of negativism, stronger than the simple need to complain, is definitely present here, and both critics and general readers noticed it.

Terkel establishes the theme that working is a very mixed blessing with the four quotations he selected as epigraphs and the way in which he juxtaposes them. (a) William Faulkner says that no man can eat or drink or make love eight hours a day, that all he can do that long in a day is work, "which is the reason why man makes himself and everybody else so miserable and unhappy." (b) In a Labor Day speech President Richard Nixon praises "the work ethic," which teaches the goodness of work, that a person is made better by working. The work ethic, "America's competitive spirit," is alive and well. (c) A passage from St. Paul's letter to the Corinthians warns that each man's work will be tried by fire. (d) A workingman in an ad for the pain-reliever Anacin says, "I like my job and am good at it, but it sure grinds me down sometimes, and the last thing I need to take home is a headache." It is immediately apparent that the signals, images, and judgments are going to be mixed.

Terkel knew from having talked with many thousands of people over the course of his career that working is central to most lives.

When an editor at *Harper's* asked why he chose to do an oral history on the subject, Terkel explained, "Sex and work are the two things that have the most impact on man."[19] He recognized, however, that while work is terribly important, it is not always a positive experience. Most of the time, in fact, it is not. In his introduction Terkel warns that because the book is about working, it is also about violence: violence to both the body and the spirit, violence mixed with humiliation. "To survive the day is triumph enough for the walking wounded among the great many of us," he added (*Working*, xi). Most working people, he had found, stand between Orwellian resignation and Luddite sabbotage. They look, mostly in vain, for meaning and a sense of immortality in their work, and the most impressive thing about them is that, though they seldom find either, they keep on looking.

Terkel was pleased, he says, to find that many slaves to work are fighting back. Older people are adopting various forms of passive resistance – absenteeism or sloppiness – while younger ones are actively questioning ridiculous orders, the work ethic itself, or the system that produced it and is in turn perpetuated by it (*Working*, xii). They may all be fighting a losing battle for pride in themselves and their work, but the ingenious methods they have invented to overcome and dissipate the pain and monotony of their work are encouraging. A woman answers the telephone with an assumed name and persona. Another fantasizes that when she leaves her job she will go to the theater and live the wonderful role of ballerina. A man lets an occasional car pass his place on the assembly line without screwing his assigned bolt tightly, imagining the trouble this will cause his company. Several men have assigned grandiose but consciously humorous titles to their menial jobs (*Working*, xiv).

Terkel makes the subject of working personal. He was dreadfully unhappy in law school, he says, as he prepared for a career he knew he would be miserable following for the rest of his life. His dread, he implies, caused him to fail (perhaps throw) the bar examination on his first try. He ran from law and its way of life, knocked about from one thing to another, and finally found in entertainment the life he preferred. He considers himself one of the fortunate few, a man who actually loves his work. It may be precarious, but it is apparently never dull.

He admits that in searching for witnesses for this subject he was at times on unfamiliar terrain. He knew Chicago when he went out to do *Division Street*. He knew the depression when he went out to do *Hard Times*. But his knowledge of the wide range of jobs he would encounter doing *Working* was limited. He implies that he did not begin his search with the hypothesis that work attacks the human body and spirit like a demon, that he came to it in the course of his interviews with working people (*Working,* xix). Whether this is indeed true is, of course, unknown. Some critics have suggested that Terkel approached the subject with the elitist assumption that all work that is unintellectual or uncreative is debilitating and found what he set out to prove.

Terkel does admit one prejudice, which he claims was somewhat modified by what he found. He had always despised the automobile, considering it at best a necessary modern evil and at worst a kind of curse. But after interviewing witnesses who make, sell, and use motor vehicles of all kinds, he has to admit that the car provides a large number of people with security and pleasure. All a car needs, it seems, is careful control and wise use (*Working,* xxi).

If America is to be healthy, Terkel concludes in his opening remarks, its people must redefine, give new meaning to, the word and activity called work. At present it is seen only as the way to make a buck. It must become a meaningful, fulfilling way to spend one's life (*Working,* xxii). The people he interviewed, while for the most part negative about their work, knew what it should be. They longed not for jobs but for vocations, the kind of work that would mean something both to themselves and to their society. They believed that their spirits were larger than the work they did and that they were capable of higher responsibilities and more demanding tasks than they were called on to do. They longed for work that requires thought, gives pride in accomplishment, and permits the worker to leave a permanent, positive mark on the earth (*Working,* xxiv).

Interestingly, Terkel told the inquiring *Harper's* editor that he undertook this project to provide a forum for people who, otherwise voiceless, considered themselves machines, mules, or robots yet knew they could be so much more. He was perhaps admitting the prejudice his critics charged and he denied in other places: that he was an elitist intellectual who considered work demeaning and in his book proved his point. Then again, perhaps this *Harper's* comment merely reflects, in hindsight, what he found. Perhaps it is both.

Working is a better-organized book than either *Division Street* or *Hard Times*. An almost-exhausting wealth of testimony is divided into nine parts, according to what Terkel considered the nine broad categories of work: (a) those who work the land; (b) those who communicate with the public; (c) those who clean and protect property; (d) those who live by the automobile; (e) those who tend to people's personal needs; (f) those who work in the minor professions; (g) those whose work other people envy (athletes, managers, the retired); (h) entertainers, publishers, and educators; and (i) people who change work midway through their careers and those who pass work on to their children. Unfortunately, Terkel does not always clarify the relationships between stories within each division, and in places we feel that he has included a witness who does not fit but whom he could not bring himself to drop. In general, however, *Working* is organized logically and clearly and is as good as this type of book can be.

Working begins with three prefaces: the first by a steelworker who calls himself "an old mule" of modern technology, a man who is tied to his job and fantasizes about being a wild and free college kid; the second by three young newspaper boys, who differ wildly in their opinion of the job, the last one concluding that it has taught him to hate printers, customers, and dogs; and the third by a mason who takes great pride in his work because stone is the earth's immortal material. These witnesses are a cross-section of and perfect opening act for the multitude of witnesses that follow.

Those who work the land run the gamut from family farmer to migrant farmworker to strip miner to heavy-equipment operator. They share a precarious existence filled with danger and guilt. There are few hints in this section of either pride or hope. The reader who does go beyond their testimony – as some, including critics, probably did not – has reason to conclude prematurely that Terkel is out to prove that manual labor is without worth or redemption.

Those who communicate with the public range from a receptionist to a flight attendant to a model to an executive secretary, then on to an actor, a press agent, and a salesman. The first group is by social definition largely female, the second largely male. A profound weariness, a yawning fatigue, hovers over both groups, even when the work they describe is not physically demanding. These people are constantly out in society, meeting people, performing services for them, and doing work other laborers envy, yet their work seems to suck their vital juices away, leaving them unfulfilled. They speak bitterly of long hours, harsh treatment from superiors, and a deep desire to be more creative. There is about them an air of pessimism, if not of downright resignation to despair.

The cleaners and watchers of real estate are what we generally call blue-collar workers. The garbage-truck driver who leads off the testimony sets the tone: "You get just like the milkman's horse, you get used to it." The first speakers, all cleaners, pick up trash, attend washrooms, and keep factories and their machines operative. The watchers are a doorkeeper, two policemen (one black, one white), an undercover industrial investigator, and even a film critic. They all maintain and keep safe from harm things owned by wealthy individuals and corporations. As the testimony moves upward to ever more responsible work, where the worker is increasingly free to do things his or her own way, increasingly respected by society, so does the sense of self-worth increase.

On the other hand, as we move upward to witnesses in more respected professions, the jobs become less secure, often more dangerous, and not necessarily more lucrative. This factor does not seem to matter, however, as long as a heightened sense of personal worth accompanies the greater respect. The interviewees here prove Terkel's contention that people seek work that is significant, challenging, and respected. Despite its dangers and the fact that it does not make people happier, more challenging work increases worker pride, the one indispensable ingredient of fulfillment.

The fourth section, which Terkel colorfully titles "The Demon Lover," features people whose work depends on the automobile. Collecting and organizing the testimony for this section caused Terkel to modify and moderate his antipathy for "the gas buggy." These men – and they all seem to be men – make, drive, sell, and park cars for a living. They force Terkel to express a grudging admiration for this body of the American work force that so completely identifies positively with a machine he always considered necessary but undesirable.

To this point *Working* follows clearly marked, logically topical lines. Section 5, which features people who serve personal needs, is a bit less cohesive than the first four sections, although it is more cohesive than some of its successors. Those who see to human appearance – a barber, a hairdresser, a cosmotologist, a dentist – do have goals that are similar to those of people who offer hospitality and entertainment – a hotel clerk, a bar pianist, an elevator operator, a janitor. They all long for respect, and even more, for control. But their goals take different paths. The first enjoy making decisions for their clients, partly because they feel they know better than their clients what is good for them and partly because they cannot stand being told how to do their work. The second long to be recognized as specialists who do "clean" work, as public servants rather than public slaves. These two groups are followed by a bank teller and an auditor, the first female and the second male, both of whom count people's money. Despite the American fascination with finance, both of them long for what they consider higher callings.

Those who serve personal needs by using their feet exhibit more physical anguish than any other group. Because they do "busy" work, they seem to have little energy left at the end of the day to enjoy their leisure hours. A meter reader and a mailman, who work outdoors most of the time, have to deal with human and animal violence. A supermarket clerk and a skycap, who work indoors, deal more with verbal than with physical abuse. But violence is violence. As a group these people claim they are proud of their work, many of them speak well of bosses, but more than any other group they talk of the need to move on to other work in order to preserve their health and sanity.

Also in the category of personal service come "just housewives," as the women who stay and work at home tend to call themselves. Here Terkel effectively contrasts two witnesses to show the range of women without public careers. One is married and has both a gainfully employed husband, who has built her a nice home, and well-behaved children. She feels guilty for spending so many leisure hours reading. She looks forward to the nearly complete freedom she will one day have when her children are grown. The other, who is Hispanic, has five children but no husband and lives on welfare. She has no hope. She cannot even look forward to the time when her children will be on their own, because even then she will have no skills to sell in the marketplace. Her insecurity has led her to despair.

Section 6 is disconcerting because it begins on a positive note, perhaps the most positive of the book, but slowly descends into pessimism. Living "The Quiet Life" are a lady who finds and rebinds, thus saving, old books, a job she finds fascinating, creative, and fulfilling; a druggist who has spent 40 years on one street corner and feels he has been amply – if not always financially – rewarded for his long work; and a piano tuner who has turned a craft into an art, a job repairing mechanical instruments into a romantic life with music. On into "Brokers" the optimism, although diminished, continues with a woman who delights in finding young families places to live. But then a yacht broker, who finds toys for the rich, says he is tired of bringing this kind of joy and talks fondly of the day he can retire. One stockbroker talks about handling people's hopes and dreams, but another argues that the market is rigged and his work superfluous. Finally, those working in "Bureaucracy" all seem to have stopped looking for meaning in their jobs, for any sense of accomplishment, for any way to contribute to the good of humanity. The only voice of hope here is a former bureaucrat who was "canned" for insubordination and now lives off handouts as he works for the have-nots of society.

In the seventh section, made up of those who are often envied by the rest of us for the glamorous lives they lead, we hear of disenchantment at the top. In "The Sporting life" a jockey describes the physical hazards of the horse races that bring crowds to their feet, races that bring him money and sleepless nights. A big-league baseball pitcher speaks of the privations and insecurities of his own sport. A press agent regrets that the sporting life he once knew and loved is dying. A woman tennis professional decries the endless travel and dependence on wealthy sponsors that her sport demands. A hockey player finds it sad that when a person is paid to play he loses his sense of the sport, the thrill of competition, the art of his skill. While these people love their work, they approach it now with doubt, dread, even disgust. The only person here who seems to be without doubts, National Football League coach George Allen, is aglow with false bravado and simplistic morality.

People "In Charge" are the envy of people who feel they are not in control of life and work, but they too say that the kind of power they exercise is not all that wonderful. A radio-television executive bemoans that he must neglect his family to stay on top of his work. A factory owner discusses how he hates being the "boss" of others, how he works alongside his employees in order to be "one of them," and how he is compelled to drive himself harder than his workers, all to make him feel worthy of his position. The head of a bank's audit department speaks of a tremendous boredom that far surpasses any sense of power he might feel. A boss who lost his job describes his feeling of worthlessness when he was pushed aside and his privileges taken away. The former head of a conglomerate explains that business is a jungle, with rewards going only to the amoral survivors of a dog-eat-dog battle. "The most stupid phrase anyone can use in business," he muses, "is loyalty. The only loyal people are the people who can't get a job anyplace else" (*Working*, 409).

"Ma and Pa Courage" are a married couple who own a small grocery store. They are their own bosses, an enviable accomplishment, and at first they appear to have a good life. Yet they tell of being victimized by petty thieves, disgruntled customers, inflation, and the police, and of the long hours they must spend behind the counter. The freedom they sought so avidly has become slavery. Their dream is to sell out and buy a resort, "where people can develop a finer awareness of theirself." It seems an unlikely prospect, but it keeps them going.

The idle rich and the retired have their say. A wealthy woman describes how the nice feeling of freedom from financial worry can quickly give way to longing for purpose in life. To be gainfully employed, she says, is essential for human happiness. A retired railroad engineer seems to live entirely in the past, when he was busy and needed, and thinks of the present only as a time when passenger trains have been derailed. A former shipping clerk, with loads of time on his hands, spends his days in the company of a shriveling group of old friends, going to fires, singing old songs, trying not to think that his glory days are over.

In the eighth section, Terkel follows the work cycle from cradle to grave. A pediatric nurse speaks of how she loves her work and how she will never retire, although we learn that in fact she has already done so. An elementary school teacher talks proudly of her achievements with the generations of kids she has known. An occupational therapist, a nurse's aide, a nursing-home attendant, a grief counselor, a grave digger – all serving the needs of people passing through the various crises of aging and death – all speak positively about their work, seem to be fulfilled, and vow never to retire. They are not without frustrations, pain even, but there are obviously more rewards working with people in need than with those who are well off – and certainly more than working with inanimate objects.

In the final section Terkel fills his stage with clumps of people who in one way or another are searching beyond their work for a sense of vocation. A former child prodigy, now simply a tree nursery attendant, deeply regrets his years as a radio Quiz Kid and talks of his need to avoid all social commitments. A carpenter with the soul of a poet worries about building houses for rich people when within sight of his work poor people live in shacks. A magazine editor bridles at having to obey mindless orders from superiors and dreams of a day when she can use her words more creatively. A commercial artist explains that he is no better than a pimp: people want trashy art, and he gives it to them. A 35-year-old who has refused to knuckle under to orders or to compromise herself says that she has worked at 16 different jobs in as many years.

These are the most rebellious but also the most hopeful of Terkel's witnesses. Many of them have changed jobs, searching for loftier, more fulfilling vocations. A salesman from the urban Northeast has become a small farmer and café owner in rural Arkansas. A successful young insurance lawyer has left a lucrative job to become a volunteer defender of the homeless: he lives on the edge of poverty, but his life and work make sense to him, and he has been rescued from the despair he once spent so much time fighting. A former television producer is now a small-town librarian and pronounces herself redeemed. A former butcher is now a sculptor who relishes his creativity. It is healthy to change jobs, to start over, to go in search of youthful dreams long abandoned, to choose meaning over monetary compensation.

A concluding section presents "Fathers and Sons" and the work they do. One pair operate a service station. The father has accepted his lot in life and is proud his son is following suit, but the son is deeply unhappy and feels he has sold himself into slavery. Another father, a steelworker, by his own description a mere cog in a vast wheel, wanted his son to be a doctor. Instead the son became a priest and now leads public protests against pollution caused by the mill at which his father works. The father cheers him on.

A son who teaches in an adult-education program recalls how his father got rich by devoting his entire life to corporate business and vows that whatever the cost he will not let himself be used the same way. A retired freight-elevator operator speaks fondly of his two sons, one a policeman and the other a fireman. He defends them against charges of corruption and negligence and tries to demolish the stereotypes that plague both professions. They are servants of the public good, he says, helping prevent social catastrophes.

The Critics

Excerpts from *Working* appeared in a number of publications. *Today's Health* carried snippets as early as February 1972, as Terkel was just beginning to edit the first interviews. *Harper's* carried selections from it as a major feature in its February 1974 issue, the month the book appeared, along with an interview with Terkel. In April *Ramparts* and the *Chicago Tribune* carried lengthy excerpts. In June *Ms.* featured women of the book. This third Studs Terkel oral history was treated as a potential best-seller from the start.

It was also widely reviewed. The influential liberal Protestant weekly *Christian Century* called *Working* "a major social document of our time."[20] Peter Prescott of *Newsweek* gave it an unusual amount of space and concluded that Terkel had himself another winner. The key to Terkel's success, Prescott allowed, was his sympathetic ear, which won people's confidence and made them want to tell their stories.[21]

Bernard Weisberger, in his *Washington Post* review, placed *Working* in the lineage of Oscar Lewis's *The Children of Sanchez*. It captured a particular people at a particular time, he said, and opened their lives for the world and future generations to observe. Weisberger did find fault with Terkel's lack of method, but for him the book was valuable as raw material. The testimony itself demonstrated profound dissatisfaction with modern life. *Working* reached deeper into the contemporary psyche than it claimed – or even knew.[22]

Charles Morrissey, reviewing for *America,* was both impressed and depressed by the pessimism he found in *Working.* He was surprised and saddened by how much workingfolk hated the way they spent their waking hours. *Hard Times* had found people laughing amid troubles, but *Working*'s people did not laugh, except sardonically. Without taking into account that the people of *Hard Times* were recalling a time long past, were able to laugh now but had probably not laughed so much then, Morrissey blamed Terkel for choosing too narrow a spectrum of witnesses, for giving only skeletal settings for his interviews, and for providing no ameliorating analysis. Still, he praised Terkel for uncovering what he considered a major social problem: the unfulfilling, impersonal, degrading nature of so much of the work Americans do.[23]

The *Chicago Tribune,* on the other hand, compared *Working* with Ralph Nader's 1972 study *The Workers* and concluded that, despite Terkel's warning of pessimistic comments, this was a far more optimistic study than Nader's. Nader had found and deplored what he called the "treadmill effect" of most work: the gradual but finally almost-total loss of zeal for the work itself, for reform, for improvement. Nader's people seemed reduced to zombies. At least Terkel's witnesses wanted to and were able to articulate their dissatisfaction. They had not abandoned hope, because they still had the capacity to think and the energy to complain. Despite their cynicism, they had not lost their souls. Perhaps their hope made them unhappy – and their unhappiness gave them hope.[24] In his *Atlantic* review later in the year Benjamin DeMott echoed this sentiment when he applauded Terkel's accomplishment: "He never misses the fine energy of the quarrel in the street, and aims always at honoring the nerve of resistance."[25]

Susan Jacoby, writing for the *Saturday Review,* called *Working* "a documentary masterpiece" and praised it for pulling away the veneer of tranquillity to reveal the startling degree of labor dissatisfaction in the nation. Terkel's witnesses, she said, ran the gamut of animosities, from boredom to degradation, and such feelings are far better aired than suppressed. After reading their comments she concluded that much of the alienation American workers feel can be blamed on company rules and regulations. To increase production workers have been forbidden to fraternize on the job, and their isolation leads to stress and dissatisfaction. Corporate snooping, employed to enforce such isolation and efficiency, only increases the dissatisfaction and anger.[26]

Marshall Berman, in his review of *Working* for the *New York Times,* looked back over the three Terkel oral histories and found a pattern. With *Division Street* Terkel had successfully revived Popular

Front literature by letting the common man speak. "The people" of that first book, however, were a bit murky, indistinguishable, and "the masses" were almost faceless. *Hard Times* had lacked focus, but there "the people" emerged from the mists to be individuals; the book provided more perspective than *Division Street* because of its broader and better sampling of opinion. Now with *Working* Terkel seemed at last to have found his legs. This was Popular Front Literature at its best. It had individuality, depth, and focus. At times, Berman said, the testimony was so hot he almost dropped the book. His only complaint was that Terkel should have given more of his own opinion, more analysis, and more of the questions he had asked to evoke such responses.[27]

Reviewer Thomas Smith suggested in *English Journal*, the monthly magazine of the National Council of Teachers of English, that *Working* should be made a classroom aid. It would demonstrate to students the relationship between a person's job and his or her self-image, Smith said, and it would serve as a fine model for showing how communication skills grow naturally from the way a person spends the workday. He pointed out that a teacher at Chicago's Old Town School of Folk Music (Win Stracke's place) was already teaching students to write folk songs based on *Working*'s stories.[28] As it turned out *Working* was adopted in many public schools, with results both successful and controversial. In one Pennsylvania school, as a matter of record, the opinion of *Working* was so strong and divided that Terkel put in a personal appearance to defend it.

Although some critics found fault with *Working*, the majority of them highly recommended it. There was really only one thoroughly negative assessment of its merits, and that from Anatole Broyard in the *New York Times*. His "Tory" reaction to "working-class" complaints ran over into two editions of the grand old paper. In the first part he expressed surprise at the negative tone of the testimony, but instead of crediting Terkel with discovering the true voice of the American worker he questioned whether Terkel was really reporting the truth. He wondered what sorts of questions Terkel had asked his people, how he had asked them, how he had edited the answers, and to what extent he let his own biases affect the people he chose to interview, the raw material for this puzzling book.

Broyard pointed out that Terkel admitted that many witnesses were surprised at reading the transcripts of their own testimony – saying they were not aware they thought and felt the things they had told him – and he speculated about the extent to which these thoughts and feelings were more those of Studs Terkel than of the common man he claimed to represent. Terkel's face, he theorized, put people in a "philosophical" mood. He probably made them act more "intellectual," which in the vernacular is translated as more "miserable." Thus this modern day "Book of Job" might well really be the Testament of Studs Terkel, armchair workingman, self-designated intellectual, self-appointed apostle to and mouthpiece for the American working class.[29]

A few years later there were hints that at least some of Broyard's suspicions may have been justified. When *Working* was adapted for the stage in 1978 several of the original witnesses were invited to attend a performance, and at least two who spoke with the press afterward said some interesting things. Mike LaVelle, the steelworker "Mike LeFevre" who appeared early in the book, was livid at the way he came across on stage as a "gorilla." He may, of course, have been reacting more to the way the director or the actor portrayed him than to the way Terkel had done so in the book. On the other hand, perhaps the "gorilla" personality merely was exaggerated by flesh and blood. Or perhaps he was inaccurately portrayed from the beginning. The hospital aide who is "Cathleen Moran" in the book and the play told reporters that she had not been entirely truthful when she talked with Terkel. He had made her believe (she did not say whether it was by the questions he asked or his tone of voice or facial expressions) that he wanted her to complain of her work, to tell a negative story about it, and she did. Her attitude toward her work could, of course, have changed during the intervening five years, but the questions her story raised were not insignificant.[30]

In his second day of Terkel-bashing Broyard said that while parts of *Working* were brilliant, long sections were repetitive, making the book sound like a broken record. He said that Terkel raised reader expectations unnecessarily high by opening with the testimony of Mike LeFevre, who made us expect all of the working class to sound like Paul Newman or Spencer Tracy. When this proved not to be the case the book began a downward plunge from which it never recovered. Broyard went on to charge that liberals like Terkel, who do not themselves work at manual labor, seem to take pleasure in making people who do despise their jobs and therefore themselves. They make themselves feel and look good by making other people feel and look miserable.[31]

Working probably deserved both the praise and the criticism it received. It is an outstanding monument to the working people of the late twentieth century, and it is a book molded by the philosophy of Studs Terkel. It is both Terkel's most far-ranging and severely limited book. While it deserves its accolades, notably its nomination for a National Book Award in 1975, it should be taken with a grain of salt.

From the time of its appearance *Working* received widespread attention, was hailed as a masterpiece of oral history, and stirred the imagination of a large audience. It sold more than 85,000 hardcover copies in its first two years; a paperback edition has now sold more than 100,000 copies. Terkel and several working people, though not necessarily the ones in the book, appeared on television's "Phil Donahue Show" in January 1977, and, in an interesting turn of events, the show was reviewed in the *Chicago Tribune* by Mike LaVelle.[32] Before the stage version of *Working* opened on Broadway in May 1978, Terkel predicted that the play would be either a smash or a disaster; it was in fact neither.[33] Nor was that the end of *Working*, either as a play or as a source of controversy.

Talking to Myself

By the summer of 1974, as *Working* worked its way up the best-seller list, Terkel was already plotting his next book. He was by this time a hot item in the literary world, and Pantheon could ill-afford for him to be idle. He had to take advantage of his hard-won fame. He had reported on the common man, and now he would turn to the uncommon. His next book would be on the subject of power.

From the start, however, the project caused him grief. He called it his hardest assignment, "my Everest. To tell you the truth, I don't know if I can do it."[34] After a long, frustrating, maddening time he found that he could not. The powerful were also the rich and famous, not his kind of people. They did not respond well to him, because they knew he did not admire them. Besides, they already had forums for their opinions and stories.

He discussed his dilemma with Schiffrin, who suggested that Terkel break his logjam by interviewing himself, that he do an oral autobiography. As usual Terkel at first questioned Schiffrin's judgment, but, again as usual, he finally agreed. He sat down with his tape recorder and began to talk. It was what he called "a bastard form of interview," one in which he did not so much interview himself as let his memories flood out as a stream of consciousness. He went on and on, as intrigued by what he was learning about himself as his readers were when the book was published. He has never said how many sessions he had with his machine or how many hours he spoke, but he filled five reels of tape, and the transcribed copy ran to almost 400 pages.[35] By 1977 he had still another oral history, this one his own.

Terkel had some doubts about the project. "I hope the book has . . . the feeling of somebody talking to you" was about all he dared hope. He was afraid he might come across as a clown, but if he did, he hoped it would be as King Lear's streetwise jester or as a classic comedian like Emmett Kelly. In fact he came across not as a clown at all but as a man who spoke of serious matters with great good humor. *Talking to Myself*, while it was witty, clever, and in places funny, was received as the work of a man serious about himself, his profession, and his world. Some have called it Terkel's best book. It is certainly his best-written book, and it is as close to an autobiography as he will write. As the oral history of America's most popular oral historian, it is a significant achievement. As the colorful memoir of one of the modern era's most colorful entertainers, it is a wonder to read.

Talking to Myself, by Terkel standards a modest book of 316 pages, is subtitled "A Memoir of My Times," and it covers the full 65 years of his life, with emphasis on the younger days. The nearest thing to a dedication reads, "Remembering the hall boys." Terkel acknowledges the aid of his "empress of transcribers," Cathy Zmuda, and of Tom Englehardt, Dian Smith, Myriam Portnoy, Jeanne Morton, and his wife and son. Finally, there comes a cryptic "To my memory, a blessing and a curse."

In an opening "Caveat" he says that this will not be a memoir in the usual sense, because it was done orally. It will have little to do with chronology and even less to do with family. He warns that his memory may have played tricks on him, but he believes that having worked for so many years with a tape recorder has taught him to be as honest as possible. He admits concealing "a private domain" of his life, a place where he will not let the public intrude, but he hastens to add that there is nothing in that domain that matters much to readers anyway. He warns that the book is "higgledy-piggledy," and we find right away that indeed it is, although not so much as it at first appears. It has its own personal logic.

There are 29 scenes in five books. Although some of the scenes appeared earlier, in slightly different form, in such publications as the *Nation, Chicago,* and *Rolling Stone,* they fit nicely into the newer material. Reading the story of his life, told by himself, allows us to follow Terkel's dynamic, sometimes illogical, always undisciplined mind over a broad landscape of hills, valleys, sharp turns, narrow passages, and wide vistas, and in the end we know that the life, if not the whole man, has been captured fully. *Talking to Myself* is another Studs Terkel success.

Book 1 follows a twisting path through a maze of swirling memories. "The Visit" takes place in London in 1962, at the flat of Ivy Compton-Burnett, the "mouselike" author. Terkel's recorder is sluggish, but at last he makes it work, and the relaxed writer explains to him that life is a mounting block for art. Terkel realizes that he learns new things only when his machine whirls, and he concludes that he and Richard Nixon are the two contemporary men most defined by the recorder.

He then remembers "Dreamland," that magical West Side of Chicago ballroom of his youth, where he would stand outside on the street to catch the sounds of jazz coming through a door he cannot enter. This was about the time he told his teacher that he wanted "Fightin' Bob La Follette" to be elected president. Then it is 36 years later, and he is telling his law school class reunion the same thing, this time provoking more derision than consternation. Nine years later he is interviewing La Follette's vice-presidential running mate, Burton K. Wheeler, for a book. He is himself still an unreconstructed Progressive, although Wheeler is not.

His brother Ben is in trouble for picking up that girl at Dreamland, and Terkel is himself picked up by thugs more than a decade later. He knows them because he attended public school with boys just like them. A high school classmate is investigated by Congress, and Terkel angers another gathering of alumni by bragging that their school has produced at least one celebrity. He saves Ben's life by telling the girl's thuggish boyfriend that their mother is ill, and 40 years later he tells Vittorio De Sica that he once lived out a scene from *The Bicycle Thief*. Now he is writing a book, following Ivy's advice, using his own life as a mounting block for art.

On the same trip to Britain Terkel interviews Bertrand Russell, "The Man Who Shook the Hand of the Man Who Shook the Hand of Napoleon." At that moment Kennedy and Nikita Khrushchev are facing each other down over nuclear missiles in Cuba, and Ben Bradlee tells Terkel much later that Kennedy would have started World War III rather than look weak. Kennedy had loved the song "Big Bad John," and, like Chicago mobster Kid Pharaoh, he preferred to die rather than yield his pride. At Lord Russell's home in Penrhyndeudraeth, Wales, Terkel learns that Russell's grandfather once met Napoleon, and Terkel realizes that in the brief moment since Elba the power of weapons has changed so dramatically that today no one can possibly win. Russell agrees.

Book 2 shifts scenes, and Terkel is in South Africa in 1963, walking amid the chaos of apartheid, talking with his black "bedroom boy" as well as to a tribal chief. Throughout South Africa he finds the faces, the voices, and the tensile strength of his black American friends Big Bill Broonzy and Mahalia Jackson. In the South African Police, appointed to preserve segregation, he sees and hears Chicago's Red Squads of the 1930s and recalls the night they picked him up on his way to rehearse one or another radical play, how he was almost throttled for boasting that he was "a citizen." He feels kinship with the black people of South Africa.

He interviews Irish Catholic activist Bernadette Devlin in a Chicago taxi as she hurries to a lecture. She tells him how a Protestant woman poured tea and kept to all the British amenities as she explained to Devlin that the Catholic church is the Antichrist. Terkel thinks how like South Africa this is, a place where social amenities are interwoven with violence to the human spirit, and he sees just how complex the creature called man is.

Book 3 finds Terkel on a Chicago city bus, where he loses the hand-painted Veronese scroll he received in 1962 with the Prix d'Italia, which he won for his radio production "Born to Live." He recalls wearing a tuxedo to the award ceremony, the first time he had worn one since he played on the old radio show "First Nighter" in the 1930s. On that show he played crooks, and now his acting helps get him safely across Italy without knowing the language or social habits of the people. He interviews and smokes cigars with Federico Fellini, and back in Chicago he finds the remains of one of these Italian cigars in his WFMT desk drawer. He remembers the boy in Italy who sold him a necktie, a boy who looked like a child in a sixteenth-century painting he saw earlier that day in a museum.

Book 4 opens at the Democratic National Convention and Chicago street riots of 1968, then moves on to remember journalist James Cameron, the first man to tell the truth about Vietnam. In contrast, Chicago's "big dumpling," Mayor Richard J. Daley, presides over Mahalia Jackson's funeral, desecrating the occasion, but no one speaks up in protest. Someone needed to ask "the impertinent question" that day, as Cameron so often did.

Terkel started asking impertinent questions back at McKinley High School, as a debater. Once he won by arguing for the death penalty, when he did not believe in it. Once he lost by arguing for Philippine independence, when he did believe in it. In the first case but not in the second he asked impertinent questions. Columnist Mike Royko asks them. Characters in the play *The Front Page* did. Which reminds him of a performance of *The Three Penny Opera*, an impertinent show, and a debate between two Chicago characters over Vietnam, where impertinence raged.

Book 5 opens with a memory of how opera singer Claudia Muzio won Terkel's heart when she sang at McKinley High. Then Terkel is himself an extra in *Carmen, Turandot,* and *Lohengrin.* Just as in 1927 he was conquered by the voice of an Italian woman, so in 1947 he was conquered by the voice of a black gospel singer. He recalls how he supposedly "discovered" Mahalia Jackson, how close they were, the night she introduced him to Martin Luther King, Jr., the way she sang at the Lincoln Memorial, and how so he mourned her death.

He is in Montgomery to cover the Selma civil rights march. The people he interviews, black and white, remind him of film actors. People feed him words, then cuff him around. He is a Yankee in this medieval land, the land from which Big Bill and Mahalia came to Chicago. He travels with Bill and sees him humiliated both by segregationists and by young blacks who do not remember or appreciate the rural southern scenery of his music. Bill is dead now too, but

Terkel sees him in the black people of South Africa. In Sweden a man tells him how grand he thinks Jackson's music is, and, finally, Terkel is back in Chicago: "I am in my mother's hotel. I am standing outside the door" (*Talking*, 316).

The Critics

In places *Talking to Myself* goes beyond oral history, beyond memoir, to the level of literature. It demonstrates that had he chosen to undergo the discipline, Terkel could have been a fine novelist, even if he had limited his stories to events from his own life.

In his review for the *Chicago Tribune* Alden Whitman mused that after reading *Talking to Myself* he would not retain attorney Studs Terkel to settle his will, the way his mind tends to skip about, but that he would certainly choose him as his defense lawyer in a capital case, particularly if he were guilty, for Terkel could be counted on to beguile any jury.[36] Robert Lekachman wrote in *Saturday Review* that before reading *Talking to Myself* he had always wondered why Terkel's people, the people he found to interview for his books, were so much more interesting than the people Lekachman himself met in everyday life. Now he understood. It was Terkel who made his witnesses interesting.[37]

Most reviewers, however, found *Talking to Myself* something of a disappointment. Nora Ephron complained in her *New York Times* review that Terkel's mind flitted from subject to subject in a blinding confusion of images, restlessly telling its muddled story, in the end concealing more than it revealed. It was not at all clear to her, though he had obviously piqued her interest, why Terkel had turned out as he had. She was frustrated by the "hiddledy-piggledy" style of his story, with its attendant continuing mystery.[38] John Leonard, in a second *New York Times* review of the book the following day, agreed that Terkel had covered up too much. By refusing to ask and answer certain questions (impertinent ones?) himself Terkel had left for his readers huge gaps and perplexities.[39]

Leonard apparently expected Terkel to bare all, which, of course, he warned from the outset he would not do. Four years later, in his review of Terkel's next book, *American Dreams*, Leonard was still unhappy about Terkel's tendency to conceal parts of himself. In describing his life as an iconoclast, Leonard griped, Terkel made it all sound too simple. He left the impression that the Red

Scare, which had cost him dearly, was no more irritating than a bit of plaque between his teeth, merely an aesthetic annoyance, something to be scraped away by using humor as dental floss.[40]

There were even harsher reviews. Richard Christiansen, offering a second *Tribune* review later the same year, complained about what he called Terkel's tendency to create "cartoon characters" instead of the kind of real people he found for his other oral histories. This book, he concluded, was a sadly ineffectual tribute to its singular subject.[41] A *New Yorker* writer sniped that Terkel needed a more zealous editor. Readers forced to plow through so much irrelevant detail, the writer piped, would be grateful if someone took a sharp pencil to the next Terkel project.[42]

Talking to Myself began as a way to help Terkel get his mind off the difficulties involved in doing an oral history on the subject of power – and perhaps to escape the feeling that he had failed that project. Judged by many critics a disjointed, perhaps even dishonest book, its literary merits unrecognized by philistines, it sold less well than other works, some of less quality. Still, it sold 22,000 copies in hardcover and 6,000 in paperback in the United States and Britain. Although less discussed and remembered than other Studs Terkel books, it could in the long run be considered his finest legacy to twentieth-century letters. It may not tell all about Studs Terkel; it obviously did not tell all that his critics and other readers wanted to know; but it tells enough about one of this century's most compelling personalities to be a great book.

Chapter Four

American Dreams, a "Good" War, and Great Divides – Social and Racial

Talking to Myself required less time to complete than any of Terkel's other books. Even as he prepared it for publication he was working on his next project. He did not do a book on power – he has never returned to that subject – but instead pursued a topic that let him work with a broader sampling of people, the kind of people he liked. He went in search of American dreams. Although some of those he interviewed dreamed of power, and some had achieved a measure of it, others dreamed of very different things. Some had reached their dreams, some had not, but they were all ready and willing to tell them to Terkel.

American Dreams

In this, his fifth book, Terkel once again acknowledges the contribution of both André Schiffrin – though this time not for the idea, just for the necessary support – and the ever-faithful typist Cathy Zmuda. He again thanks Nordstrand, Pellegrini, Baum, and Unrath of WFMT for their considerable help; again he mentions "scouts" who helped him locate his subjects, drove him places, introduced him to people and places – men and women from Chicago to Kentucky and the Carolinas to Mississippi and California and the Northwest. He had visited more than 200 people, from a wide swath of the nation, and more than half of them were represented in this book of their dreams.

Again Terkel denies and disdains any concerted attempt to find consensus, balance, or statistical proof of information regarding

American dreams. He says he searched only for the truth by which his witnesses ordered their lives. Again using the jazz simile, he says he improvised, simply asking people to recount their dreams, and followed the melodies and rhythms they offered him. It mattered not to him whether the dreams they told him had been or ever would be realized. Dreams are dreams. He provides brief settings for his witnesses, just enough for us to know who the person is, but again he includes few of the questions he asked. His conclusions, such as they are, are found only in a brief introduction. He refuses to bow to the wishes of his critics.

There is about this book a somewhat negative tone, perhaps established by Terkel's elaboration in the introduction of his mother Anna's failed dream, perhaps also by opening the testimony with a cynical former Miss USA and a disillusioned Chicano immigrant. Throughout the book there are more broken than realized dreams. Terkel does ask his readers not to overlook the positive signs to be found in these pages: a growing tendency for Americans to air their grievances; the chances many have taken to change their lives for the better in middle age; and the dreams of liberty and equality that continue to grow amid so many painful reversals of fortune. Lesser and unfulfilled dreams may dominate the field, but great and realized ones bloom in the desert.

Terkel does an impressive job of organizing his 470 pages of testimony by 100 witnesses into subject headings that divide and in part conquer what otherwise would have been a daunting, perhaps even oppressive task of reading. There are two "books" placed between a prologue and an epilogue, and the classification of dreams, with their creative titles, is the best job of this kind Terkel has done. If *American Dreams* is not his most widely read, respected, or rewarded book, it is his best organized. Terkel has at last perfected his art.

What Terkel discovered, captured, and offered up in print about Americans and their dreams, both lost and found, is most revealing. It begins with sadness. Miss USA ridicules the common dream of being a beauty queen because she has lived it and knows its emptiness. A Chicano ridicules the dream of America because as an immigrant he knows that it too is empty. Bosses describe their struggles to fulfill dreams of financial security and of power, both of which bring the burdens of responsibility, the fear of losing what has been won, competition with themselves, the trauma of being fired, and the consequences of being labeled unsuccessful. Their dreams too seem empty.

"Onward and Upward" takes the story further. A corporate troubleshooter, a man of some power, at first says blandly that "the American dream is to be better off than you are." Then after reflection he admits that one never really feels he is better off than before, that he always wants to have and be more, to climb and stand higher up the ladder (*Dreams*, 38). An American Indian explains that for him and his people the dream is "in the past, understanding who you are instead of looking to the future" that holds no promise (*Dreams*, 50). The daughter of a Hollywood movie producer concludes that the dream is all fantasy, that it is interpreting one's existence through images on the silver screen, living out what she calls "the Jewish revenge" on America (*Dreams*, 52). For one of those silver-screen images, Joan Crawford, the dream has been fulfilled as she spends time with her loving children, one of whom was at that moment plotting to write one of the most scurrilous of the "get even with famous Mummy" books.

For some people the dream is by its very nature elusive. A woman who collects autographs is never satisfied; she cannot be, for she must always search for just one more signature. For millionaire communications magnate Ted Turner, who finds it so easy to make money, the dream is to win the National Basketball Association championship.

Newcomers to America speak. A Finnish immigrant tells Terkel how he came here for a chance to be somebody and ended up working his life away in a coal mine. A black Tennessean recalls coming up from the South, to the real America, a place of freedom and equality, only to live in fear of its violence. A descendant of John Adams, recalling his family's history, concludes that the reason they never got rich is that they kept to the American dream of liberty for all. An Italian immigrant who has made it big in America contends, "The system is all right. Most of the time. The people who run it are no good." He does not include himself in the critical assessment (*Dreams*, 102).

A Polish-born Jew, living in Los Angeles, finds at age 94 that she has realized her American dream: she has lived almost a century, has constantly been intellectually challenged, and still has all her marbles. For Florence Scala, the heroine of *Division Street,* the dream of fighting the "progress" that destroys neighborhoods is never-ending yet still fulfilling. A second generation Yugoslav-American remembers her life as one of the early women to participate in labor strikes and says that by still being alive, still able to dream of better days ahead, she is content. A son of rich parents says with a sigh that the poor are richer than the rich because they still have dreams, and the words of a Puerto Rican bellhop seem to bear him out: "I guess I'm gonna have to hit it big" because up is the only way to go (*Dreams,* 126).

A new immigrant from Austria, a novice actor named Arnold Schwarzenegger, says that his only goal is to make it big in America. For him the American dream is to get rich and always want more. A maintenance man who came from Latvia in 1956 says that while he has fulfilled all the dreams he brought with him he now lives in fear that blacks will take his dream world away from him. A Cuban who arrived in 1971 vows his love for America despite not having fulfilled his dream of becoming one of those rich Americans he once read about in *Life* magazine. A Greek immigrant, recently arrived, tells Terkel that he believes this is "the one country in the world where you can do anything you want so long as you don't bother anyone." He is about to join the U.S. Army in order to gain citizenship (*Dreams,* 135).

Once again Terkel talks with people who live off the land. A Tennessean has found his dreams fulfilled in owning property and raising his own food. A California migrant farmworker, however, is striving in vain to feed, clothe, and house her children. A Japanese-American couple, recalling how they were taken from their farm and sent to an internment camp, conclude that the American dream is for whites only. And an American Indian woman says that when land is "given forever" to her people it is given only to the point when a white man wants to take it back.

A white Appalachian coal miner's wife says that America will never be a land of dreams again until the poor are given an equal chance to dream once more. In contrast, a storekeeper in the mountains of eastern Kentucky believes it is possible for people still to beat the moneyed interests and enjoy the fruits of their land and labor. A black Mississippian who went through the fires of early voter registration describes a dream in which all Americans realize that they are brothers, but he says that until they do he plans to keep his gun loaded. A former exalted cyclops of the Ku Klux Klan details how his racial attitudes changed as he worked with a black woman on an economic project for the poor of both races and how he now dreams of racial harmony and cooperation. This last man impressed Terkel more than any other witness, and he still describes to his audiences how one man – and thus human attitudes – can change when given the chance.

"In the City" Terkel heard different dreams. There they are tinged with misgivings. A cab driver expresses pride in the way his family has realized so many dreams of prosperity over three generations yet feels angry that he himself is still a member of the working class. A former convict proudly describes how he works to keep young people free of criminal records, yet he knows the odds he faces and admits that sometimes he feels his dream is "an illusion" (*Dreams*, 225). A cop believes that he has realized his dream of performing a public service yet indicates that the dangers he faces each day are beginning to drag him down emotionally. A successful wrestling promoter describes how a mean wrestler makes more money than a clean one and calls the American dream "a hype, an elusive nothing" (*Dreams*, 235). Ed Sadlowski, recently elected head of a local steelworkers union, faces the fact that organized labor has lost its sense of mission, that it no longer goes into neighborhoods to bring a little culture to "the working stiff" it should represent (*Dreams*, 242).

Terkel then tries to demonstrate that dreams of public service are not always illusory. A photographer has had the courage to fight the mayor and city hall over urban renewal and the president and the White House over Vietnam. An elderly woman who was once an intimate of notorious mobsters demonstrates that people her age can face an uncertain future with courage and confidence. A gay rights advocate in Mississippi, a nurse in Chicago, a man who has no family left – all of them keep on working to make a difference in a difficult world. A quiet Catholic housewife, provoked into activism by social problems she sees around her, speaks of dreams in terms of human potential. A woman up from Tennessee, recalling how back on the farm people rang a bell to sound alarms, speaks of dreams in terms of waking people to dangers.

In book 2 the dreams become more specific and personal. John Howard Griffin, author of *Black like Me*, the story of a white man who traveled the South as a black man, concludes his story by saying, "If we take people as they are, we tend to make them worse. If we take people as they could be, we can get better" (*Dreams*, 281). A California radio commentator, joking about his eternal optimism, quotes a friend's description of his dreams: "You could be found in a raging torrent, in a canoe upside down, lose your paddle, and still say we're gonna prevail" (*Dreams*, 288). A woman who grew up in the utopian community of Arden, Delaware, mourns the demise of that dream of a perfect human society.

A president of the Daughters of the American Revolution says the American dream is to love one's country. A successful physician dreams of better health care for the poor he serves. A woman living in poverty dreams of a time when her children can live anywhere they wish. A race-car driver dreams of winning the Indianapolis 500. A black professional football player dreams of the day when he no longer has to get up early on Sunday mornings to pump up his hostility for opposing teams. A Chicano businessman says cynically that the American dream is born of fear, the fear of losing what one has gained, that nightmare which goads a man into working even harder. A woman of some wealth says she has found the American dream "too goddam much work." A couple who won $1 million in the Illinois lottery hope that there is no reincarnation because they would hate to find themselves living at a lower level, now that they have found their dream. A 95-year-old author who has built his own wilderness house portrays the dream as "to keep your head above water and to do your share in making the dying society as tolerable as possible" (*Dreams*, 330).

"They Also Serve" begins with the dreams of politicians. Liberal Senator from South Dakota James Abourezk, who has decided not to seek reelection, tells Terkel that he dreams of a time when power is no longer in the hands of a few rich men. Conservative senator from North Carolina Jesse Helms, claiming that America cares for human welfare better than ever before, dreams of a day when we will truly return to the free enterprise system. Cleveland's young controversial Mayor Dennis Kucinich, predicting a war between big companies and the little people, says he dreams of a day when the nation will be run by the ideals of Thomas Jefferson rather than IBM. Italian-born

Chicago alderman Vito Marzullo glowingly describes the American dream of being able to work and earn as much as one has the capacity to make. Detroit's black mayor Coleman Young says he knew he had reached his American dream when he returned as mayor to the church he had attended as a "colored" boy and was treated as a king. But the black night watchman who caught the Watergate burglars at work seems to have no dreams, just ongoing duties.

Voices from the media are also heard. Husband-and-wife crusading newspaper editors from eastern Kentucky speak of duties as well but seem to relish both the condemnation and the praise their work brings them. The editor of *Soldier of Fortune* dreams of maintaining and enhancing the prestige of the armed forces. The editor of *Rolling Stone* dreams of fighting oppressive authority wherever it is found in American society. The struggling young editor of a new daily paper dreams of someday having control over his own destiny, of being able to speak his mind, of having an effect on society.

Young dreams are many and varied. A fundamentalist Christian dreams of saving souls. A Hare Krishna convert dreams of saving himself. A former Republican party public relations man who has left politics now dreams of finding a solitary place to tend his own garden. An actress from a liberal home, having given up social activism, dreams of the day she will return to the streets to demonstrate. A young man who cannot adjust to the competitive society in which he finds himself yet is not "crazy" enough for state assistance dreams of social and financial security. A successful lawyer is "bullish" about everything American. A man raised in a conservative home in a conservative New England town has led an attack on a nuclear power plant and dreams of a time when protesters can live without intimidation and fear. He longs to see a flood that will sweep over Washington and restore power to the people.

In his epilogue Terkel juxtaposes a former logger who now works to save American forests and an elderly black man who attended the March on Washington in 1963. They provide an appropriate ending for a book on dreams because in old age they still work for the betterment of humanity, because they believe in the future, because they still dream.

The Critics

American Dreams is not a tidy book. Its voices do not always come across clearly. Its various themes are not always in focus. Despite its intelligent organization, with all its clever titles, it is an enormous ball of multicolored twine, ready to unwind. Yet it is a powerful book, with many articulate dreamers, and it will be read, studied, and pondered by generations to come. It will help explain this present age and its people by showing men and women of the future how and what we dreamed.

The book received a great deal of attention when it appeared, during the election year of 1980, as the "Reagan Revolution" was slowly gathering strength. It reflects deep frustrations with things as they were and a desperate search for alternatives. Alan Miller of the *National Review* paid Terkel the compliment of comparing him with Alexis de Toqueville roaming the countryside in search of the American spirit.[1] The success of Terkel's search was confirmed by Richard Kuczkowski of *Commonweal*, who concluded his comments about the book by saying, "Terkel knows where to find America."[2] The *Christian Science Monitor*'s Roderick Nordell, equally impressed, called Terkel a master interviewer, with an "art that conceals art."[3] John Leonard of the *New York Times*, who four years earlier had not cared for *Talking to Myself*, complimented Terkel this time around for being such a skilled listener and editor. In this book, Leonard said, Terkel had stopped making bad jokes and had emerged as our contemporary Walt Whitman (Leonard, 29).

Robert Sherrill, writing for the *New York Times Book Review*, called *American Dreams* "a dark-hued book of frustrations and disappointments" but also found in it a number of hopeful signs. Although times were still hard for many Americans, they seemed on the verge of doing something to improve their lot. Terkel's witnesses, he said, were saucy, scrappy, and ready to tackle problems, both their own and those of the nation at large.[4] Thomas Gannon of *America* called it a positive sign that the powerless – the poor, the elderly, the racially and economically exploited – had such a champion as Studs Terkel, who knew how to give them and their articulate if not always grammatical opinions a national forum.[5] Lawrence Goodwin of the *New Republic* called Terkel America's "most authentic populist minstrel,"[6] which is exactly what he longed to be.

There were dissenters. Barbara Grizzuti Harrison, writing for the *Nation*, criticized *American Dreams* for its lack of focus, an element she blamed on Terkel's having chosen a topical question so broad that it defied clear answers. She was further frustrated, as critics of Terkel's earlier books had been, that he refused, except perhaps by his choice of witnesses and the way he edited their answers, to "come out of the closet" and express his own opinion about the material.[7]

Helen Epstein of the *Washington Post* agreed that the book lacked focus and cohesion and that it had no real unifying theme. She was also disturbed by the lack of evidence that Terkel's people thought before they spoke. The book would sell well enough, she granted, not because it was a good book or had anything valuable to say but because it was by Studs Terkel. Terkel was an author widely discussed and respected but rarely read. People liked the idea of Terkel, the optimistic populist, the folk historian, more than they knew or understood either him or his people.[8]

John Lahr, after spending five full *Harper's* pages on *American Dreams*, concluded oddly enough that it was nothing more than an extended daydream, hardly worth reading.[9] Peter Prescott, in earlier times one of Terkel's great admirers, said in *Newsweek* that Terkel had to feel somewhat guilty as he continued to make best-sellers out of the confidences his people gave him free of charge (Prescott, 118). He apparently did not know that Terkel compensates his speakers.

American Dreams sold well – 82,000 copies in its American hardcover edition – and was translated and distributed abroad in German, Japanese, Russian, Bulgarian, Finnish, Danish, and Dutch. It added greatly to Terkel's fame both at home and abroad. He entered the 1980s richer, more famous, and more influential than he had entered the 1970s. He had published five best-selling oral histories. Yet he was plagued by nagging questions: Why did his books not have a clearer focus? To what extent was his testimony authentic? Why did he not provide more analysis and opinion? Was he a real oral historian or merely a literary talk-show entertainer? While the questions would not go away, they did not deter Terkel. His most ambitious and successful book was on its way.

"The Good War"

André Schiffrin and Pantheon anticipated that Terkel's sixth oral history, "The Good War," would be a great success. The first hardcover printing, released in October 1984, was 125,000 copies. This proved a conservative figure, and more printings were required. It became a best-seller and won a Pulitzer Prize.

Terkel dedicated "The Good War" to James Cameron, author of Point of Departure, whom he called a "master of his trade." Once again Terkel credited Schiffrin with the idea for the book, and he listed a legion of traveling companions, "who were cicerones as well as chauffeurs," and scouts who helped him locate and meet his witnesses. The title was suggested by World War II news correspondent Herbert Mitgang, but Terkel chose to place the title in quotation marks "not as a matter of caprice or editorial comment, but simply because the adjective 'good' mated to the noun 'war' is so incongruous."[10]

He added a subtitle, which actually appears above the title on the frontispiece: "An Oral History of World War II." He had used the phrase "oral history" only once before, for Hard Times, and it would appear that he viewed these two books – rightly – as different from his others. While all his books contain oral testimony, these two deal with specific historical events and thus fall into a different category from that of books dealing with a city, a way of life, and dreams. Still, this is not an ordinary oral history. Once again Terkel makes clear the difference between "memory" and "hard fact and precise statistic." This is not straight history, or even oral history in the usual sense, but a book of memories about World War II: Terkel history.

"The Good War" was Terkel's most widely read and in many ways his most powerful and influential book. He features 120 witnesses, mostly under their real names this time, in 589 pages of testimony, most of it focused and vivid. The introduction is Terkel at his best, containing both a survey of what is to come and a brief analysis of what it means. Again the analysis is too spare to satisfy his critics, as are the questions he sprinkles among the answers his subjects gave him. For many readers there is still not enough Terkel, but he has apparently chosen to stick with a successful formula, and it proved a hit.

Having a central theme, a clear subject matter, gives *"The Good War"* a tighter focus than most of Terkel's other oral histories. The witnesses, socially and geographically diverse, are well chosen and their testimony well edited and organized, although as in earlier books Terkel occasionally includes testimony that does not quite fit because he apparently considered it just too good to discard. Overall, however, the mural of World War II that he paints with his human oils is complete and satisfying. It forms a collective memory, a full-bodied oral history, of the one American war that seemed then and for the most part seems still to have been justified, if like all wars, essentially tragic.

"The Good War" is divided into four "books," each filled with the memories and words of people who participated in the war, plus an epilogue of comments by people too young to remember but whose lives are still deeply affected by it. Part 1 of book 1, "A Sunday Morning," recalls 7 December 1941, when the Japanese bombed Pearl Harbor and the United States was compelled to enter a war that had in other parts of the world been raging for as long as four years. A Hawaiian who saw the first attack, then served in the army for four long years, describes his realization at the war's end that all the fighting had settled nothing. Mainlanders speak of the fear that Japanese ships and aircraft would attack California, that Japanese-Americans there would support them, and comment on the way these people were interned.

Two former barracks mates at Fort Benning tell of meeting again by chance after 40 years. This "Chance Encounter" revives memories, and each man recalls the war in Europe: the black-bordered photographs in German homes, the dogmeat local people had to eat, the Russians who were first introduced as friends and later branded enemies. The Europe they knew in those days was half impressionistic art and half devastated planet. It is clear from their words the extent to which those who molded American life for the next half-century were themselves molded by the war.

"Tales of the Pacific" captures the memories of five naive young Americans who were sent to fight the Japanese. The war in the Pacific seems to have changed the raw kids sent there more than the one in Europe did. The most impressive and memorable testimony here, perhaps in the entire book, is that of Eugene B. (Sledgehammer) Sledge, a combat marine who fought his way across the Pacific. He returned after the war to pursue a childhood interest in ornithology and became a professor of biology at Alabama's Montevallo University. As one of World War II's most articulate and objective participants, he was also featured in Paul Fussell's *Atlantic* article "The Real War, 1939-1945" in 1989.[11] Sledge sums up his memories by telling Terkel that "there was nothing macho about the war at all. We were a bunch of scared kids who had a job to do" (*"Good War,"* 59). In his story are details of how decent American kids were made into trained killers.

Men who served on ships in the Pacific tell a somewhat different story. They may have been in constant danger of dying – Terkel entitles one section "Reuben James" for the ship that carried its entire crew "to the bottom of the sea" – but because they did not come into hand-to-hand combat with the enemy, they tended to think of the war as a grand adventure. Most of them still consider the war more exciting than frightening, and some even seem to wish they could relive it. All of them tend to agree with the man who says, "My world view came from sailing the sea in World War II" (*"Good War,"* 107).

In the section "Rosie" (titled after the stereotypical war-plant worker Rosie the Riveter) American women who experienced the war back home remember the days of fear and longing. They were left behind to make the instruments of war their men used to fight the enemy. Some worked with chemicals that turned their hair a frightening shade of orange and made breathing difficult; some lay awake nights worrying about husbands who might not return to them; some had to cope with husbands who returned alcoholics. They admit, with a bit of embarrassment, that the war brought them business and professional opportunities that would not have come in peacetime. They demonstrate that the women's movement some 30 years later was born in the man-shy 1940s. Not one woman, not even a WAC or an army nurse, calls it a good war. Unlike the fighting men, women were not even permitted to think of themselves as crusaders. They seem to have seen through the propaganda, including war films, better than the men. Many of them were persuaded by industries committed to restoring the "traditional" family to return home and be housewives when the war ended, and this delayed the women's movement but did not end it. Women remembered.

There was, despite E. B. Sledge's disclaimers, a great deal of machismo during the war, some of it genuine, much of it manufactured. One man who refused to cooperate in the war effort was imprisoned and branded a coward. Another volunteered to fight for democracy, did so with distinction, then learned to his dismay that he had been fighting to prop up corrupt regimes like that of Chiang Kai-shek in China. A man who is now a gay rights activist went through the war pretending to be straight, playing football with the guys, and serving as a chaplain's assistant, only to be detected and saddled with a dishonorable discharge.

Book 2 begins with high-ranking officers, an admiral and a general. Once more the difference between land and sea warriors is obvious. The admiral, who confesses that he found the Pacific war boring, is now cynical about the war that was meant to save the world from barbarism. He is distubed by the militarism that has now been institutionalized, indeed that runs our foreign policy. He cannot even bring himself to watch films of World War II. "We steal the lives of these kids," he sighs. "They don't die for honor and glory of country. We kill them" (*"Good War,"* 193). The general, on the other hand, is more convinced now than when he was a young officer that America must keep its military force strong for the good of the free world. He is sorry the American people in general no longer believe we have a mission to perform in the world. "I'm certainly not warlike," he says rather unconvincingly. "Blessed be the peacemakers. But somebody's gotta take care of the peacemakers while they're makin' peace" (*"Good War,"* 197).

The memories of those who were children in the war have particular poignancy. In "Growing Up: Here and There" are a London boy who lived through the Blitz; a Japanese girl who remembers hunger more than danger; a German high school student who recalls going directly from classroom lectures about Hitler's greatness to a British prisoner-of-war (POW) camp; and a Russian boy, now a poet, who recalls walking to school through mountains of snow, all alone because his mother was too weak from hunger to come with him.

By contrast, a California girl remembers inventing foreign invasions because no real ones ever came; she now regrets her town's postwar population explosion more than its wartime losses. Another California girl, from Oakland, recalls the wonderful array of army boyfriends the war brought from the military bases to her front door.

A Jewish boy whose family escaped Europe and made it all the way
to the American West Coast remembers it all as one big adventure
because his family kept him ignorant of the dangers they faced along
the way.

The beginning of the war's end – what Churchill called the end
of the beginning – was D-day, the Normandy invasion of 6 June
1944. One of the invaders, among the first waves of American troops
to reach the beaches, remembers living a lifetime that day and yet
being so absorbed in his work that it was his third day in France
before he remembered to be scared. He says now that when some
people seek power, others die, and too few make a protest (*"Good
War,"* 264). A black tank instructor recalls the joy in his battalion
when General George Patton ordered them into battle against white
Germans, and he ties the war in which blacks helped defeat a nation
that claimed racial superiority to the civil rights movement of the
following decade. His thesis is confirmed later on in the testimony of
a black pilot and a black war correspondent. Another black veteran
recalls the way American forces were segregated and how blacks
were hanged for having sex with European women, but he also
recalls how his bitterness melted as he saw the Statue of Liberty on
his way home.

A woman recollects how she lost her husband in the war, then
met and married the buddy who had watched him die. Her second
husband muses about why his friend died while he himself lived, and
he speculates what the family photographs in his home would have
looked like had things gone the other way. A Jewish army surgeon
describes how he felt treating Nazi officers and how all of Europe
smelled to him of death. And Maxine Andrews of the Andrew Sisters
recalls the disbelief, then the relief, then the joy of soldiers when
during a show she read the announcement that the war was over.

Book 3 features people who in one way or another profited from
the war, helped conduct it, or reported it for the news media. This
section, as with sections in some of his other oral histories, seems
held together more by force of Terkel's will than by logic. Yet as with
other such mismatched sections, it has solid impact. "Sudden
Money" is about a foot soldier who learned how to make and handle
money in wartime and used what he learned to become a postwar
investment broker; the citizens of a small town transformed into a
bustling metropolis when the U.S. government decided to build LSTs

there; a man whose building-contracting business was perfectly equipped to take advantage of war needs and make him filthy rich; and a man whose food market paid him ever-higher financial dividends as wartime shortages drove prices up. For these people the war was not a hardship. For them it ended the Great Depression.

"The Big Panjandrum" presents a few of the "pretentious personages" who ran the war. Thomas G. (Tommy the Cork) Corcoran helped FDR win reelection in 1940 and then was put in charge of procuring energy for the military complex. John Kenneth Galbraith held control over wages and prices and virtually dictated the direction of the domestic economy for four years, emerging from the war as the nation's most influential economist. Congressman Hamilton Fish opposed entering the war until Pearl Harbor, then led the fight for Congress to declare war on Japan. Virginia Durr, the liberal Alabaman, was the subject of FBI surveillance because she had Japanese friends. Despite the responsibilities, burdens, and worries these people carried, they seem to agree that the war was the best time of their lives. They had a mission to perform and the power to perform it. They stood for something, they did their duty, and for the rest of their lives they were respected.

"Up Front with Pen, Camera, and Mike" features people who used literary, artistic, and thespian talents to aid the war effort. John Houseman recalls his work as a propagandist for the Office of War Information. Henry Hatfield describes making radio broadcasts to German citizens, encouraging them to give up. Cartoonist Milton Caniff describes the way his comic strip "Terry and the Pirates" went to war against imperial Japan. Bill Mauldin speaks somewhat shamefacedly of how his cartoon "Up Front" with the celebrated Willie and Joe made him famous and rich, at the expense of the American boys he portrayed. Playwright Garson Kanin discusses the way the D-day landing was filmed for maximum dramatic effect, and Richard Leacock does the same about the filming of battles in Burma. Photographer Walter Rosenblum recalls the way German soldiers tried to surrender to him, although he was not a combat officer, as he followed the advancing American army through France.

Book 4 is the longest of the books, nearly 200 pages, with the most witnesses, 36, and it is both the least well organized and the most dramatic. It brings the war to a ragged, climactic close, describing in vivid detail those final days. "Crime and Punishment" features a military policeman who found it hard to keep American soldiers from going AWOL to avoid the last futile skirmishes; a black sailor who contends that it was pure carelessness that cost the lives of 200 black ammunition workers at Port Chicago in 1944 in an explosion later judged the most deadly home-front accident of the war; and American James Sanders, who compares memories with German Hans Gobeler about the night Sanders's ship sank Gobeler's.

In "A Turning Point," a series of vignettes on crucial moments in people's wartime lives, an American remembers meeting the Russian allies at the Elbe, the smell of lilies near the water, his hopes for world peace, and his desire that he someday be buried there. Russians describe their defense of Stalingrad, the defeat of the German army, and feeding German POWs, the very men who had tried to kill them.

In "Chilly Winds" an American prosecutor at the Nuremberg trials recalls the moment when he realized that Nazis were not monsters, that normal human beings could be trained to commit atrocities, and that this was even more frightening than seeing Nazism as an abberation of human nature. An American intelligence officer recalls using Nazis to gather information and learning that his own government was helping some of them escape to South America; entering death camps to find prisoners starved by those Nazis; and returning home to find Americans hunting Reds instead of Nazis. A commander of the American volunteers in the Spanish Civil War, the Abraham Lincoln Brigade, remembers how he was castigated during the postwar McCarthy era for having been a "premature anti-fascist." Terkel's wife, Ida, here once more speaking as Eileen Barth, describes how when she and others refused to wear silk stockings in the late 1930s, to protest Japanese aggression in Asia, they were branded the same way.

Perhaps the most moving of these stories is told by a man of mixed parents, a German mother and a Liberian father. Because of the man's color, the Nazi government denied him admission to the Hitler Youth and to schools of higher education. He survived the war, despite his open hostility to the regime, and finally achieved Liberian citizenship. His indictment of the German people for following Hitler and then claiming they had no choice is as poignant as his indictment of the American army for not denazifying German society when it had the chance.

"Is You Is or Is You Ain't My Baby?" is the song Jacob Bronowski heard coming from an American ship as he roamed the ruins of Nagasaki after the atomic attack. For Terkel this song and Bronowski's moving account of the devastation caused by the bomb ask, What of the future? A nuclear physicist describes how he worked on the bomb, sure that it would save the world, then quit, convinced that the arms race must end if the world is to be saved. A mother of two children with birth defects says she knows that working at Oak Ridge caused her tragedy. An Indiana farmer, a member of the crew on the plane that dropped the bomb on Nagasaki, explains that he simply accepts what he did because otherwise "I could drive myself whacky" (*"Good War,"* 53). An army chaplain based on Tinian when the bombs were carried away to be dropped on Japan, who did not at that time question the morality of dropping them, now travels the country as an itinerant "Peace Pilgrim" protesting war.

Finally, as in his previous books Terkel collects the thoughts of people too young to remember the war. In "Boom Babies and Other People" an American girl recalls how she and her friends had to learn of the war and its horrors from books. A pair of young Germans say that with better education their generation now knows not to follow leaders into another war. Most of these young people, however, wonder whether they will live full lives or be killed in a nuclear holocaust. Their testimony stands in marked contrast to that of a World War II veteran who seems to sum up the feelings of older people: "World War Two? It's a war I still would go to" (*"Good War,"* 573).

The Critics

"The Good War" received widespread attention from the time of its publication in the summer of 1984. The July edition of the *Atlantic* featured excerpts from the stories of E. B. Sledge, Debbie Hahn, Elliott Johnson, Tettie Bassie, Dempsey Travis, Richard Pendergast, John Houseman, Maxene Andrews, and John Smitherman. The *Chicago Tribune* carried a similar sampling in October.

Reviews were for the most part favorable. Terkel and his books had won a place in American letters, and this new one was judged a worthy addition to the collection. Some of the comments were effusive. Garry Wills said that Terkel had broken through to the great, previously untapped memory bank of the common people concern-

ing this most important period of American history.[12] William Goldstein, reviewing for *Publishers Weekly*, called the book a living mural
of faces from the war, a lasting achievement.[13] James Kaufmann of
the *Christian Science Monitor* applauded Terkel's knack for eliciting
such intimate reminiscence and simple eloquence from his people.
"The difference between regular history and Terkel's oral history,"
he wrote, "is like the difference between reading a boxscore and
actually seeing the game. There is life here, not statistics."[14] And
Loudon Wainwright in the *New York Times* welcomed the immediacy
and empathy he found in the book, concluding that Terkel seemed
never to have interviewed a man he didn't like.[15]

There were, of course, a few complaints. Even Wainwright,
despite his praise, admitted that the book had a few dull spots, some
repetitions, and several passages that needed abbreviation. Another
New York Times review, by Terkel's old nemesis Anatole Broyard,
raised doubts about the validity of some testimony. Broyard suggested that some of the witnesses were caught up in "retrospective
excitement" and had embellished if not downright invented parts of
their stories. He pointed to one man who admitted in his testimony
that he was perhaps overstating matters and suggested that if this
man knew as he spoke that he was exaggerating, it was probably true
and to a greater extent for many others.[16]

Questions like those Broyard raised were somewhat muted during the first few months as *"The Good War"* became a best-seller and
in the spring of 1985 won a Pulitzer Prize. Uncertain how to classify
it, the Pulitzer committee named it best of "General Nonfiction."
Terkel had invented a new type of literature, one all his own. As
always, he was hard to categorize, hard to force into a mold.

Naturally, the *Chicago Tribune* gave the Pulitzer award front-
page coverage, with a story and photograph of Terkel, commenting
that he was being honored for keeping his ears and his heart open to
the common man.[17] The *Nation* said in a similar vein that he was
rewarded because "he reproduces the vox populi unfiltered (though
skillfully elicited and edited)."[18] In response to all the attention and
accolades Terkel was unusually self-deprecating. "If you stick around
long enough, anything can happen – look at Reagan," he teased. "I
didn't think I had a chance."[19]

The announcement of the Pulitzer Prize did not meet with universal approval, even – perhaps particularly – among Chicagoans.

John Blades, editor of the *Tribune*'s "Book World" section, inter-viewed a number of "Chicagoland" critics who, having perhaps been reluctant to take on a local folk hero before, surprised some people with their comments. Blades began his story by conceding that Terkel was a popular choice for the prize, that he was a local icon, a populist who had earned a niche for himself by celebrating the opinions of the common man. On the other hand, Blades said that he had often heard people in private question the validity of Terkel's "oral history." Did Terkel, whose questions and interpretations were so rarely and briefly printed, unduly influence his witnesses and their testimony? Did he choose speakers who agreed with him? Did he edit the stories to suit his unstated theses?

Blades suggested that some Chicagoans were afraid to criticize Terkel publicly for fear of retaliation, that others admired him and what he stood for too much to make their doubts public. If asked, however, a surprisingly large number offered some rather severe criticism of his methods and results. One man who refused to be identified told Blades that Terkel really did not deserve the prize: "He got it for being Terkel, the abiding pseudo-cultural character, whose shallow and predictable politics are overshadowed by his barroom charm." John Epstein, an English professor at Northwest-ern University, said openly that Terkel's books, for all the attention they received, were downright boring. After 80 pages of *Division Street,* he claimed, even a Chicagoan who was interested in the sub-ject found it repetitive. All Terkel's books mirrored his left-wing poli-tics, and while he pretended objectivity he was in truth plugging his own ideology. Epstein called Terkel a "virtuecrat," one who places all virtue in a fictional common man created in his own image.

Robert Remini, a professor of history at the University of Illinois in Chicago and winner of the American Book Award for his biogra-phy of Andrew Jackson, told Blades that Terkel's books were not really history, not even oral history, because they offered no analysis or interpretation of data. He considered Terkel a skilled interviewer, a noble chronicler, but not a historian. His books were valuable to historians, however, because of their raw material, which he did not question. Historians owed Terkel a nod of gratitude for all he had found and captured, but they were unlikely ever to vote him into their fraternity.

William McNeill, professor of history at the University of Chicago and then-president of the American Historical Association, told Blades that Terkel should be regarded as a bard, a great and talented entertainer, but not as a historian. He admitted that unfortunately few historians are entertainers and that by enticing people to read oral testimony about past times Terkel was performing a valuable service to the profession. He guessed that Terkel let his ideology compromise his work, that he chose his witnesses and edited their testimony to substantiate his presuppositions. Still, McNeill applauded Terkel for popularizing the field of history.

Author Peter Collier, who has written chronicles of the Kennedy and the Rockefeller families, told Blades that so long as readers were aware of exactly what Terkel's books were and were not, they could read them without being taken in and could profit from their revelations. He believed too that Terkel let his left-wing biases affect his work, his choice of witnesses, the questions he asked them, and the way he edited their responses but noted that Terkel had performed a great service to the world by making a type of oral history into an art form read by millions of people. All his readers had to keep in mind was that they were reading not history or even oral history in the strictest sense but Terkel history.

Out of a sense of fair play, or perhaps of anticipated reader reaction, Blades asked Terkel to respond. His answer to the criticism was "So what?" He had heard it all many times before; it had not made him change, nor would it in the future. What is important when someone picks up a book, he said, is that he or she learn or feel something he did not know or feel before: "I don't care what form the book takes. I don't care what means it takes. But if it's able to tell a person, here's what it was like to be a certain person like myself, the reader, living in a certain time during the depression, during World War II. If I can get that in a book, that's what it's all about."

He was angered, however, by the charge of bias, by the accusation that he let his ideology influence his choice of people and the way he used testimony. "I put my thoughts in the introduction," he told Blades, "and that's it. If I were to put words in someone else's mouth, if I only offered my own political point of view, then everything I've done isn't worth a damn. You can throw the book in the ashcan, and that's where it belongs."[20] Terkel either did not understand the criticism or chose to ignore it. His summary denial and dismissal were not enough to still the suspicion that he used oral history to grind personal axes.

One person came immediately to Terkel's defense. Mike Royko, whose own testimony about the war was prominently displayed in the book, offered a sarcastic *Tribune* column against the critics. The names of "the professors" who denigrated Terkel's achievements need not be mentioned, Royko sniped, because no one would recognize them anyway. Of course the English teacher found Terkel's account of the war uninteresting – he would have preferred a novel about an English teacher with writer's block who goes to wartime France and meets this gorgeous . . . well, you know. Of course history professors considered the book unscholarly, because no self-respecting historian talks with anyone living, and besides, historians consider anything that is not dull a sham.[21]

Even when we consider that Royko is at heart a satirist and that his column is admittedly opinionated in a peculiarly Chicago manner, this piece is an unpleasant, philistine echo of old Colonel McCormick's celebrated professor-baiting. Although Terkel himself despised McCormick and what he represented, he too has often described "professors" as an essentially dull breed, except for the ones who bring him to their campuses and credit him with inspiring the work they are doing. Terkel and academia have always shared an oddly symbiotic relationship that is mixed with the ever-present odor of grapeshot.

Despite its critics and their reservations, *"The Good War"* was a financial success. To date it has sold more than 182,000 hardcover and more than 251,000 paperback copies, nearing the half-million mark all told. It has been translated into Swedish, Danish, Dutch, Norwegian, German, French, Russian, and Japanese, and all of the translations have sold well, as has the British edition.

The Great Divide – Society

By mid-1985, as detractors and fans alike continued to ponder the implications of Terkel's Pulitzer for American letters, he was himself busy preparing for publication his next book, *Chicago*. A personal tribute to his hometown, it was a rather modest effort that received modest attention. Completed and published within a year of its inception, it did not interfere with interviews for Terkel's next two oral histories, both about great Americans divides – the first social and the second racial.

Terkel had long been aware of and long warned about America's divisions. Throughout his career he had called attention to divisions between blacks and whites, privileged and deprived, haves and have-nots. He had also been intrigued by people's memories and the way they interpreted their past, as well as their dreams for the future. *The Great Divide* (1988) – subtitled "Second Thoughts on the American Dream" – is Terkel's sixth oral history (eighth, if we count the two in which he did the talking himself); in it he combines memory with dreams to probe the nature and effects of social division.

In 1985 Terkel began working on the book, which, with only 439 pages, proved a bit more moderate in size than *"The Good War."* It had 90 witnesses, though, and the complaint that it was too long and repetitive was once again heard. *The Great Divide* captured America and its people in the latter half of the 1980s, a time future historians will doubtless find highly significant, a time when Vietnam was at last discussed openly, when people voted for Reagan and opposed his policies, when the government piled up the largest debt in American history, and when social classes were growing farther and farther apart.

Terkel dedicated *The Great Divide* to Lucky Miller. Once again he acknowledged debts to transcriber Cathy Zmuda (this was her last book); colleagues Pellegrini, Nordstrand, and Baum; and Pantheon's Schiffrin, Wachtell, and Morton. Terkel listed "scouts" who helped with leads and contacts. The page of acknowledgments in fact demonstrates the continuity of his work. Topics change but technique does not.

As with Terkel's previous books *The Great Divide* contains no analysis or interpretation, but its introduction is perhaps more careful, thorough, and honest than those of its predecessors. Once again Terkel disclaims any attempt at statistical exactitude or balance, going as far as to quote from James Cameron's *Point of Departure* that balance and objectivity are of less importance than truth and that the reporter whose technique is informed by no opinion lacks a serious dimension. Following which he perhaps factitiously quotes William James: "Resign the care of destiny to higher powers, be genuinely indifferent to what becomes of it all and you will find that you gain . . . the particular goods you sincerely thought you were renouncing."[22]

Here, however, Terkel is more open than in previous works about what this book is going to say: that American society is strongly affected and perhaps even threatened by the nation's deep divisions. In an opening note he says that the Rockies, geographically separating east from west in North America, symbolizes a chasm in American society: between haves, have-nots, and have-somewhats; between classes and races and visions of America; and between political and religious loyalties, "rendering unto Caesar what may not be rightfully his and unto God what may not be spiritually His." The great American divide, which fractures into these various fissures, has cut us off not only from each other but also from our own selves, for "it is the breach that has cut off past from present" (*Great*, note).

Terkel says that while doing the interviews for this book he was burdened with doubts more disturbing than any he had experienced while doing earlier works. He became aware that Americans are losing their memories. Previously he had found "lapses, blockages, forgetteries," but people had at least been able to depend on a core of vital memory. In the late 1980s, as computer banks grew fatter personal memory banks seemed to be growing leaner. He found a widespread amnesia, "a collective Alzheimer's Disease" afflicting the American populace, a "Law of Diminishing Enlightenment" at work (*Great*, 3). He took as his main task here not the discovery of facts – a dull kind of work best left to pollsters – but the responsibility to "Dig a Little Deeper," as Mahalia Jackson's gospel tune had it. He decided to dig out and bring to light the long-buried, inchoate, inarticulate, but still beating American heart.

He was discouraged not just by the loss of memory, as he heard workingmen damn the unions that had won the benefits they now enjoy, but also by a collective loss of imagination, the capacity to solve problems. He was disturbed by the attitude of winners to losers, treating them not as victims to be pitied and rescued but with contempt, as if they deserved their suffering. He found little compassion, little discomfort in the presence of pain. Yet paradoxically he found – amid all the apathy and prejudice, the loss of memory and imagination – a surprising amount of energy, an unwillingness to surrender, and a determination to fight back against the odds. Things were happening out there, along the divide, in this confusing land-scape, things strange but exciting.

With "Situation Fluid" Terkel describes the condition he found. An "old American tradition, with new twists" was reasserting itself. "Grass-roots movements, with techniques learned from the sixties, have never been more flourishing. Most of their foot soldiers had nothing to do with anti-Vietnam protests, and yet they learned from those protests how to challenge today's Big Boys" (*Great*, 15). Terkel made their stories central to his book, with others serving as ballast and garnish for them. *The Great Divide* is Terkel's most con-sciously ideological book since *Division Street: America*. At long last, as friends and foes alike had encouraged him to do, he was speaking his mind.

The Great Divide has two parts, without titles, without any real logic, except perhaps to demonstrate the divide. Within the two parts, however, the colorfully titled subdivisions make good sense. Book 1 opens with "School Days," stories about how kids in the 1980s are being educated. A teacher of high-achieving white teenagers describes their mind-numbing conformity and how easy it is to persuade these young television watchers to believe anything he tells them.

A teacher of inner-city black children describes how difficult it is to involve in the learning process kids who feel they have no part in the myth of American history. A college art instructor decries that his students of political-cartooning have no sense of history, a point confirmed by a man who speaks regularly to college audiences. He had recently been asked by a student reporter to distinguish between J. Edgar Hoover and Herbert Hoover. On the other hand, some witnesses say that today's students are more interested in ethics than ever before, and many graduating seniors say they are voluntarily taking a pledge to investigate "the social and environmen-tal consequences of any job" offered to them (*Great*, 40). Student protest has not died; it has merely changed.

A college teacher from Arkansas speaks of students who say coldly that anyone with AIDS deserves to die, then weep when they are shown a film about its victims. Where there is no hope of rescu-ing a person, he concludes, there can be no generosity, only sorrow. Terkel found in this man's story a key to young people in the 1980s, and he often uses it as an example when he speaks to young audiences. It seems always to evoke a positive, cognitive response. Terkel concludes this section with stories about how freedom of speech is being threatened in public schools by parents frightened that their children will learn things that harm religious faith. A group of students from Girard High School in Pennsylvania, where Terkel went during the school year of 1982 to confront a protest against his book *Working*, discuss foul language and whether it should be banned. John T. Scopes remarks about how little the public school system has advanced since the days in 1925 when he went on trial for teaching Darwinism in violation of a Tennessee state law. An elementary school teacher says she cannot decorate her classroom walls with pictures of Halloween witches, the Easter bunny, or Santa Claus for fear of retaliation by the fundamentalist Citizens Organized for Better Schools.

"Family Circle" attempts to define the American family of the 1980s. Terkel finds couples separated, children working at more menial jobs than their parents, and many people falling behind in the race to get ahead. A young black woman, the unmarried mother of two, describes in graphic detail the stigma of living on welfare and blames Ronald Reagan for making it "very accepted to be a white bigot" (*Great*, 67). A "gray-collar" couple, decrying the death of the middle class, condemn people who survive "on the dole." Although they say that 80 percent of poor blacks who receive welfare need it "because there's something wrong with 'em," they firmly believe that the other 20 percent are "pullin' the wool over the government's eyes" (*Great*, 73).

Once again Terkel visits the "Family Farmer," whose condition has generally worsened during the 1980s. A farm activist tells him that a great ignorance of history contributes to the problems in the heartland. A father who is careful with his money because he remembers how the depression made him a slave fails to warn his son about what can happen and watches him make the same mistakes he himself made 40 years earlier. A midwestern farmer makes it clear how easy it would be to develop a fascist movement on the Great Plains as he rails against Zionists, blaming them for the plight of the American farmer. A young lawyer discusses her sense of fulfillment as she helps farmers keep their land while her law school classmates grow jaded piling up money at corporate law.

Even the farmers who fight bank takeovers successfully, those who are planning to stay on their farms for life, say they do not want their children to be farmers. There is despair in the voice of an activist, the daughter of one farmer and the wife of another, as she recalls the day when she and her group were denied access to U.S. Department of Agriculture offices in Washington because they were branded troublemakers. On the other hand, a wealthy futures dealer across the divide says from his Manhattan office, "Without loss, no one can win. Unless you have losers, you cannot have winners" (*Great*, 115).

"The Golden Calf" continues the story of people who, like the broker, have made it in America, people on the rich side of the divide. A stock consultant raised in a socialist home argues, perhaps too stridently, that at heart he is a radical, although he voted twice for Reagan and believes that "It's not the obligation of the government to provide something that people aren't striving to get." A career woman speaks of the "high" she gets from making a "kill" in the stock market, her lack of concern for the "Joe Blow" who is killed, and her unwillingness to trust the people in her office.

A former advertising whiz kid discusses the only kind of American poverty that disturbs him: his shortage of time. It is easy to make money in America, he says, but it is hard to make time. A woman who writes advertising copy admits that she works at her job only for the high pay, which in turn she finds unsatisfying and usually gives away. Business is where the money is, says another career woman, and that is why all the smart people end up there instead of being teachers or social workers.

Still, Terkel finds a gnawing desire among the money-makers to be of service to humanity. For one man real estate is the perfect compromise: he makes good money selling houses, while helping people find homes. He believes in the "trickle-down approach" to both finance and social service (*Great*, 148). But a doctor describes how difficult it is these days for anyone to be a general practitioner, the only kind of doctor who really knows his or her patients and can treat the whole person. The high cost of equipment has forced doctors to specialize and join large firms. Being socially involved has become so hard for most people to afford that it is considered a luxury (*Great*, 154).

From gold merchants Terkel turns to "Hired Hands," skilled and not-so-skilled laborers. Walter Reuther's brother Victor laments the decline of organized labor but admits that over the past few years it has failed to communicate its ideals to the younger generation. An older steelworker concludes that the younger men have no idea what they owe labor activists of the past, that they have no sense of history, and that this is why they are losing benefits. "I'm workin' harder, makin' less money, got less of a future," he says (*Great*, 175).

A caterer who delivers lunch food to scabs admits sadly that he is a mercenary for the big bosses, indeed a strikebreaker, a traitor to his fellow workers. But the bottom line, he says, is that he has to make a buck. A sports reporter who covered the National Football League strike of 1987 says that the mail he received on the subject was overwhelmingly in support of the rich owners and their scabs and against the legion of battered entertainers. Still, Terkel discovered a heartbeat for labor. A "Save Our Jobs" committee is thriving in one city. In another an organization of labor lawyers, fighting antilabor policies and judicial units established by the Reagan administration, carries on. Theirs is not an easy task, for as one laborer says, "There's not gonna be any middle class too long. You're either makin' big bucks or little bucks" today (*Great*, 197). The epiphany of this section is a discussion between a husband and wife: he a TWA pilot who sides with management, she a TWA flight attendant on strike. The future of labor hangs in the balance. Labor's family, like this marriage, is divided.

Book 2 is more loosely woven than book 1, and in places Terkel seems to be reaching rather far for unifying themes. One theme that does hold things together is religion, a subject he had trouble probing in earlier books but by 1988 is all the rage. God is now in fashion. Fundamentalist theology has merged with technology, and a new mass movement is under way. It is more diverse than it appears, and there are great divides across its surface. While in the main conservative, it displays some surprisingly liberal agendas as well.

New churches, like Willow Creek in suburban Chicago, are growing like mushrooms. Willow Creek's affluent, upwardly mobile members voted for Ronald Reagan over the "Christian" Jimmy Carter because, they argue, this is not a Christian world and the nation needed a tough leader. They fear no nuclear holocaust because they are bound for heaven. Their pastor, who is chaplain for the Chicago

Bears football team, claims that his church doors are open to everyone, but he hedges when asked about membership for homosexuals.

Conversely, another such modern church, with a similar membership, believes Christians have a duty to oppose unjust government policies, both at home and abroad. This church is breaking federal law by harboring Salvadoran refugees. Lutheran Pastor Richard Neuhaus, who in the 1960s was a radical but now calls himself a neoconservative, considers the members of this church criminals. They are using the refugee issue to make Reagan look bad, he says, to disrupt his Latin America initiative.

Religion also plays its dramatic part in the abortion issue, which by the late 1980s was a major source of social division in America. A group called Justlife is against abortion but, unlike other such groups, is also consistently against war, nuclear development, and the death penalty. A Catholic doctor who says he has never and can never perform an abortion admits that he can no longer sit in judgment on doctors who do. A Christian grandmother named Jean Gump is serving a prison sentence for attacking a nuclear silo. Her action, which she says was to preserve the future for her grandchildren, came appropriately enough on Good Friday.

Moving to America's racial divide – which he would explore in greater depth in his ninth book in 1992 – Terkel has a successful black career woman speak of the loneliness she feels because so few of her own people share her way of life. She is convinced that the Reagan years have spawned a new form of racism in the country. Two men who rode "This Train" to Washington in 1963, a grandfather and his grandson, discuss this new racism. The older man says whites have grown tired of "giving" equal rights to blacks. The younger man predicts that the 1990s, like the 1960s, will be a turbulent decade: "There's going to be an eruption of anger among people who have played the game and feel that they are still shut out. It's going to be a world thing" (*Great*, 283). His prediction would come true in 1992, when a Simi Valley, California, jury acquitted five police officers who were videotaped beating motorist Rodney King.

In "Neighbors" Terkel presents racial and ethnic tensions at grass-roots level. A Chicano speaks of trying to open white suburbs to his people. A Klansman protests that he should no more be labeled racist for being proud of his whiteness than Jesse Jackson for celebrating his blackness. A black news correspondent explains that the reason poor blacks do not put much stock in dreams is that they know "they're gonna be dashed" (*Great,* 295). A homeowner speaks of unscrupulous realtors who play on racial fears to gain control of property and resell it for nice profits. Owners of a ma-and-pa tavern bemoan the loss of discipline among the young people of their neighborhood. An Appalachian girl raised in a big northern city and no longer sure of where she belongs asks where home is when the heart is divided.

"After School" explores the working world of the young. Here too the divisions in American society are apparent. Some of the witnesses are college graduates who must choose between enriching themselves and working to improve society. Some are laborers, cornered by lack of skills, threatened by alien racial and ethnic groups. A young flight attendant (making a second appearance) says that if her union loses its bid for higher wages, she and her friends will simply reduce their efforts and let the company suffer. Almost all of these young people believe that protests against economic injustice must and will continue, if not on the front pages then quietly behind the scenes, and that America will slowly change for the better. Agreeing with them, a "postgraduate" leader of the Gray Panthers says that older people are certainly not about to surrender until they make the powers that be treat them with justice.

On her side of the great divide stands a young Chicago socialite. She happily recalls giving teas to raise money for Reagan and being rewarded with a briefing on the noble work the government is doing in Central America by a handsome young marine named Oliver North. She has dedicated her spare time to raising money for conservative causes, holding out her "Tiffany cup," or, as she describes, it "panhandling" for the Right. She assures Terkel that she learned all about protesting against injustice when she was a student at Sarah Lawrence College (*Great,* 364).

A former Texas congressman who lost his seat because he openly opposed single-interest powers in his own district argues that America's great problem is our loss of old-fashioned, healthy skepticism. Illinois Congressman Philip Crane certainly shows no signs of skepticism as he defends Reagan policies right down the line. A nuclear physicist who learned to be so skeptical that he felt obliged to resign a lucrative job with the government explains that most people simply do not want to face the truth. Many of his colleagues privately sympathized with his dilemma, he says, but none was willing to jeopardize comfort to follow him in his protest.

Terkel returns to religion, to Lutheran pastor Douglas Roth, a skeptic who spent time in jail for organizing his rust belt parishioners to protest the fiscal policies of the Mellon Bank. Defrocked by his bishop, he continues to speak out, predicting that America is rapidly moving toward a police state. Richard Neuhaus, a fellow Lutheran, questions the wisdom and even the sincerity of Roth's protests. One of Roth's former parishioners, however, describes with simple eloquence the agony and ecstacy of joining the courageous pastor in protest – and in jail. The great divide spreads even among the clergy, separating church administrators from parish priests.

Finally, in "Younglings" Terkel presents the strong if at times inarticulate opinions of the 1980s generation. There is talk of widespread apathy among them but also of "die-ins" to dramatize the dangers of nuclear war. One kid talks admiringly of the heroes in the movies *Top Gun* and *Rambo* and says that all he wants is his own business, plenty of money, and ease in his old age. A college freshman is already making good money and knows how to be rich within ten years, but he says he might well give it all up for a career in foreign service. A long-haired throwback to the 1960s says that his aim is to change the world. A Wharton business student who says his hero is J. R. Ewing of the television series *Dallas* explains that he is taking a course in ethics so that he can get rich without running afoul of the law. A young denizen of Terkel's own neighborhood, Chicago's Uptown, says that he is learning just enough social skills to help him survive. The great divide extends into the foreseeable future.

It would seem that the coming generation is not very different from that of the past or present. For most of this century, perhaps from our national origin, Americans have been divided along social, class, ethnic, and religious lines. So far the divisions have not been fatal, but the future promises no guarantees. Terkel does end his story with hope, with Jean Gump and her husband, both serving prison terms for attacking nuclear silos. These two grandparents, who gave up their freedom to save their descendants, are examples Terkel leaves for "Younglings" yet to come.

The Critics

Judgments of *The Great Divide* were mixed. In his review for the *Chicago Tribune* Willie Morris called the book Terkel's most ambitious and perhaps his best book; he called Terkel a nonfiction John Dos Passos.[23] Marilyn Gardiner in the *Christian Science Monitor* advised presidential candidates Michael Dukakis and George Bush that if they really wanted to understand the issues, the real concerns and dreams of the American people in 1988, they should forget the pollsters and analysts and read Terkel. He had a pipeline to the American heart.[24]

On the other hand, even Gardiner had some complaints about *The Great Divide*. The way Terkel juxtaposed his various witnesses made the book appear contrived and confused the reader, Gardiner wrote. She also felt that he chose as speakers too many white, blue-collar males, the kind of people bound to agree with Terkel on the issues. Mel Elfin, writing for the *New York Times,* called the book a morality play in which the saints, the little people, took on Reagan's sinners, the big boys. This was "a religious tract, not political fact," Elfin charged. He said that Terkel had lost his old capacity to listen, the very quality that had made his earlier books so valuable. He was no longer an oral historian but now merely a calculating advocate of liberal ideology, marshalling handpicked witnesses who would help him score his points. Elfin advised Terkel to come out of his closet and get the fresh air.[25]

Jacob Weisberg, reviewing for the *New Republic,* hit Terkel even harder. It was true, as Terkel said, that Americans care little about history. But, he argued, neither does Terkel. Paying him what for Terkel would be the ultimate insult, Weisberg likened him to Ronald Reagan: both men, according to Weisberg, have built dream worlds on vague memories, surround themselves with heroes who confirm their prejudices, and bask in the pale sunshine of fictional nobler times; both constantly rediscover the America they want so much to find.[26]

Regardless of whether Terkel had lost his knack for listening and become more advocate than historian, whether he was living in an anti-Reagan dream world with soul mates to fan his prejudices, *The Great Divide* is more ideologically loaded than Terkel's earlier books, in both its choice of witnesses and the way their testimony is organized. It has without doubt a stronger populist coloring than the books that came before it, with the possible exception of *Division Street*. But it was precisely the kind of book many of Terkel's critics had been calling on him to produce, and his public apparently approved of it. *The Great Divide* sold 61,000 copies in hardback in in the first year of publication, and Avon bought the paperback rights. It has been translated into German, Danish, and Japanese, and a British edition is, as of this writing, in the works.

The Great Divide – *Race*

Terkel was not finished with American fissures at the start of the 1990s. His next book, *Race: How Blacks and Whites Think and Feel about the American Obsession* (1992), was an oral history about the great American racial divide. The "obsession" is, of course, the division caused by race. Because Americans constantly think about it, judge other Americans by it, and pattern their lives around it, Terkel felt the subject deserved a book all its own. And, appropriately, *Race*, like *The Great Divide*, came out in an election year.

Published by The New Press, a just-established, not-for-profit house headed by Schiffrin and staffed, for the most part, by former Pantheon editors, *Race* brings back a few of the people who spoke with Terkel years earlier about a variety of topics. In fact, Terkel had worked on the book, in one way or another, for 30 years; some of the witnesses were first interviewed in 1965. But many new voices are introduced: in all, 78 people discuss 30 topics in the book's four parts. Although Terkel interviewed Latinos, Asian Americans, and American Indians, his central focus is on blacks and whites.

Terkel's people talk about how race affects friendship, jobs, neighborhoods, education, and family. A cabbie's summation struck Terkel as particularly salient: "No matter how much education you may have had, the prejudices you were taught come out. These sinister forces are buried deep inside you." Terkel acknowledges the disturbing way whites have tended to speak in code – "You know why," "You know where I stand" – and concurs with the cabbie, "they're deep, these sinister forces."[27]

Race is pessimistic, recalling old injustices and tragedies, concluding that in the past quarter century the races have moved farther apart instead of close together. The pessimism is, however, interrupted now and again by a few tales of warmth and understanding – as when an ex-Klansman finds himself working as a union leader with his former arch-enemy, a formidable black woman. At the book's end a young black man, Lloyd King, is about as hopeful as anyone Terkel can find when he says, "Maybe America . . . is in its adolescence. Maybe we're driving home from the prom, drunk, and nobody knows whether we're going to survive or not. I am guardedly optimistic – definitely guarded. If everything is going to hell, it would be hard for me to get up in the morning. But I can't honestly say, 'Sure, things will get better.' We might not make it home from the prom" (*Race*, 403).

The book conclusively demonstrates that, as he neared his eightieth birthday, Terkel had not lost any of his talent for finding witnesses, provoking them to talk, and organizing their words into a coherent, enlightening volume. *Publishers Weekly* found little to criticize in *Race:* "The reader comes away with greatly expanded understanding of much recent American social history and a wish that more respondents could display the balance of the well-adjusted mixed couples whose testimonies end the book."[28] *Mother Jones* editor Douglas Foster, writing in that magazine, called *Race* "an eloquent, extensive exploration of the national obsession. . . . Reading it is the equivalent of holding up a mirror."[29]

Race appeared in the spring of 1992, just as riots erupted in Los Angeles and other parts of the country after the Rodney King verdict was delivered, and the social tension much of its testimony described – such as a young black middle-class musician's contention that "I don't know one black person who's never had an encounter with cops" – has seen its implied consequences borne out. As the causes and aftermath of the riots became, for a couple weeks at least, the nation's obsession, network news programs included Terkel among their rosters of authorities on race relations: he said he was not surprised by what had happened; he had been listening, he understood.

Chapter Five

The Celebrity Stage

Studs and Ida Terkel have long lived in Uptown Chicago. Terkel's neighborhood, he writes, "has halfway houses, nursing homes, and all the United Nations' anonymous representatives, as well as Appalachians, Ozarkians, and Native Americans. And bag ladies of course. Unfortunately, poverty is its lot, though there is spirit enough for fifty neighborhoods" (*Chicago*, 120). He adds, with a hint of guilt, "I live on a have street in a society of have-nots. It is no more than a hundred yards away from the action, yet it is a planet distant" (120).

Whatever his misgivings about Uptown and his own place in it, Terkel loves it. He says he would not live in a downtown highrise or out in the suburbs. Uptown suits him. Because he cannot drive, he takes the 146 express bus to his WFMT offices in the Loop on Wacker Drive and back home each day. WFMT itself has moved up in status and address, to the ultramodern Illinois Center. Terkel hates the center as much as he loves Uptown.

While the center has been called "visionary" and "a positive force" in the drive to "revitalize" downtown Chicago, Terkel publicly calls it "grotesque" and has said, "It's a perfect example of humanoid architecture." As he treks from his bus stop to his office through an underground corridor, he sometimes shouts, "Zombie Canyon!" and other times whistles off-key. No one seems to notice, no one shows surprise, and Terkel says this proves that graceless architecture is so dehumanizing that in its shadows no behavior is considered aberrant.[1]

Despite his opposition, written and spoken, to Chicago's urban renewal and ugly new edifices that have replaced the old charm, Terkel still loves his city, and in his half-century career there he has laid as much claim as any other of its citizens to the title "Mr. Chicago." His radio and television shows, his public appearances, his various social crusades, his books, and his constant physical presence around town have made him as recognized, popular, influential, and powerful as any of Chicago's myriad politicians, clergy, and entertainers. "Chicago *is* the world," he once told a college audience, as he was explaining why he seldom feels the need to go far beyond its city limits to collect testimony for his books on the human condition. It is certainly Terkel's world.

Peter Prescott's 1980 *Newsweek* portrait of Terkel, "The Great American Ear," gives a marvelous account of an evening on the town – Chicago – with Terkel. As Terkel roamed the city, visiting old buddies in familiar bars, always buying the drinks, listening to stories, telling his own, and sharing jokes and folk wisdom, it became ever more evident to Prescott that the man and his town were one. At the end, when Terkel found he had spent all his money and had no way to get home, a friend who carried a gun gave him a ride, promising affectionately, "I will protect you." It was a fitting climax to an extraordinary evening (Prescott, 120).

A public figure with Terkel's recognition and influence naturally develops a taste for speaking his mind. People want to hear what he thinks, what he loves, and what he hates, and he learns to enjoy telling them. In 1988, for example, he took the opportunity when interviewed by *TV Guide* to offer a plan to reform American political campaigns. Ban all political commercials, he huffed, give all candidates equal free television time, mandate lengthy debates, outlaw polls, and fire the pundits.[2] He was particularly critical of cute, razor-cut commentators. "The bomb's not going to kill us," he said. "Pollution's not going to kill us. Neither the bang nor the whimper's going to kill us. Cuteness is going to kill us. We're going to die of cuteness" (Townley, 2).

Television, he explained, makes life appear easy when in fact it is growing ever more complicated. Politics as it is portrayed and analyzed on television oversimplifies issues, packages candidates, and spoon-feeds falsehoods to voters. Political pundits, with their glib superficialities, are "simping" America (Townley, 5). The irony of Terkel's diatribe is, of course, that he himself has been seduced by the most superficial of media. He has made television appearances – an outgrowth of his willingness to submit to newspaper and radio interviews – and has learned to give quick, easy answers to complex questions. To a degree he would not like to admit he has become a pundit.

Terkel has for a long time spoken out against what he calls America's "cult of personality." He has written perceptively about how men like Mayor Richard Daley and Kentucky Fried Chicken king Harlan Sanders were raised to the level of celebrity. Celebrity does not require intelligence, virtue, or even accomplishment – just recognizability. Recognizability has in fact replaced the criteria of wealth, class, birth, and achievement as the American way of choosing and honoring "royal" figures.[3]

The irony of all this is that by his own recognizability Terkel the hater of "celebrity" has himself become a celebrity. By championing the common man, he has become the exception, the uncommon man. In a 1981 *Esquire* article facetiously called "Commoner than Thou," James Wolcott named Terkel America's best-known barroom philosopher. Under a cartoon showing Terkel, with wild hair and a cigar, sidling up to a bar rail to have a talk with "Uncle Sam," Wolcott teased, "Salty tears fall into Studs's beer as he listens, listens, listens." Unkindly, Wolcott declared that Terkel's unfocused books, called by generous souls oral histories, squat like flabby ogres on bookshelves, unread but still puffing the fame of their maker, who fancies himself "Keeper of the Flame for the Cult of the Common Man." This is the same cult, he wrote, that has given celebrity status to Arthur Miller for *Death of a Salesman*, Frank Capra for *It's a Wonderful Life*, Sylvester Stallone for *Rocky*, and even Bruce Springsteen for *Born in the USA*.[4]

While this sort of put-down is both mean-spirited and excessive, it is nevertheless true that Terkel enjoys his fame, his celebrity, his honorary title "Minstrel of the Common Man." His old music partner Win Stracke once commented, "It's not accidental that he has the name Studs. He does have a tendency to dramatize himself." When asked about the money his books have brought him, Terkel once said that while he likes the booze and cigars royalties can buy, he wants more: "My ego is bigger than that." What he wants most, this unreconstructed socialist, is to dramatize the plight of the downtrodden and shoot down the balloons of the "big boys." To do so requires celebrity, but to want celebrity requires more than concern; it also requires ego.

On the other hand, there is a grand scheme for social reform in Terkel's sometimes shameless self-promotion. Mahalia Jackson once remarked, "He just isn't a guy that plays up to the big shots. . . . The big ones are self-sustaining. Lots of people don't know how to help themselves, don't have the knowledge. That's the kind he helps" (Koch, 86). To help that kind Terkel has sought the spotlight and used it to dramatize their plight. He has been successful at doing so because he enjoys the spotlight. Happily for him – and for the needy – his two passions complement each other. It is significant – it is proof of his authenticity as a person – that his fame has not spoiled him, that he remains as accessible as ever to friends and the needy. Still, he is a celebrity, like it or not, one of that crowd he holds in such contempt.

Celebrity encourages its holders to make clever comments, and Terkel has become a clever commentator on affairs social, literary, musical, and political. He has presided with ruffles and flourishes, making witty, relevant comments, at jazz and folk festivals. He has served as judge for the National Book Awards' contemporary-affairs category.[5] He has accepted honorary degrees from Knox, Grinnell, and Carthage, among other schools, and has many times been honored by his alma mater, the University of Chicago. Despite his reluctance to express his opinions in the oral histories, he serves as resident pundit for virtually anyone who asks.

For more than 15 years Terkel has been in the news, receiving awards, being asked his opinion on a variety of questions. In 1975 he won the A. J. Liebling Award, given by *More* magazine, a monthly devoted to the appraisal of news gathering. At its fourth annual "counterculture convention" at New York's Commodore Hotel, its editors praised Terkel for following the tradition of I. F. Stone, a man of undisputed integrity who was dedicated to truth. Terkel accepted without demur.[6] The *Chicago Tribune* had started that year by choosing Terkel as one of the 10 prominent figures it asked to name one thing that promised a bright future. Terkel had said he was most excited by what he saw in organized labor, where young steelworker Ed Sadlowski had just won a rank-and-file victory over the old guard.[7] And the *Tribune* ended that year by choosing Terkel as one of the 12 leading figures it asked to define the major characteristic of the old year. Terkel said it was a new awareness. Americans had become aware, in the year following the Watergate hearings and

Nixon's resignation, that the voice of authority is not always the voice of morality.[8]

In 1976, the year of America's bicentennial celebration, Terkel appeared before the Senate Foreign Relations Committee to discuss the question of whether Americans do or do not care about their nation's foreign affairs and why or why not. As Terkel spoke the committee's members came and went and made it clear that they were interested in neither the question nor Terkel's answer. Considering himself someone whose opinions were worth hearing and heeding, Terkel at one point complained about "talking to leather" instead of to senators. But trooper that he is, he went on to tell the press and the *Congressional Record* that average citizens "don't give a damn because they feel no one gives a damn about them." He spoke eloquently, if only to leather at the moment, on behalf of the common man, of the gulf between government and citizenry.[9] Only a celebrity would have been asked to give his opinion.

In 1977 Terkel was again in the national news when he joined 60 other prominent Jewish leaders to sign a statement supporting the American Civil Liberties Union's defense of free speech for members of the American Nazi party.[10] In 1982 the ACLU gave Terkel its Bill of Rights Award for his appearance in Girard, Pennsylvania, to defend the right of a teacher to have her students read his book *Working*.[11] Also in 1977 he joined a group of liberals who decided to purchase the *Nation* magazine. They chose 26-year-old Hamilton Fish III, the mirror opposite of his ultraconservative grandfather, to be their publisher and Victor Navasky to be their editor.[12] The younger Ham Fish, despite deep personal and ideological differences with his grandfather, was in 1982 able to arrange for Terkel to interview old Ham for *"The Good War."*

It was also in 1977 that Terkel made enemies in his hometown by appearing in a 45-minute German television documentary about Chicago. He told his important foreign audience that Chicago was the most racially divided large city in the Western world, and he placed most of the blame for this situation at the feet of recently deceased Mayor Richard J. Daley, who, he said, had confirmed segregated patterns with acres of concrete barriers. Quoting Daley's slogan "Chicago Is the City That Works," Terkel agreed that it did indeed work – for wealthy corporations and contractors.[13] To say such things, particularly to outsiders, particularly to foreigners with money to invest, was considered an act of disloyalty, both by professional Chicago boosters and by a lot of average citizens. Still, this was Terkel speaking, and even those who felt he had made a mistake tended to take it better from him than they would have taken it from others. Terkel was known to be completely loyal to the people of Chicago, an enemy of the power structure, and, of course, a curmudgeon.

Terkel could never lose with the Chicago populace or his fans across the nation. One moment he was garrulous, the next lovable, and they accepted him for whatever he happened at the moment to be. The same month he appeared on the German television program, in his garrulous pose, he published in *Vogue* a lovable account of his trip in 1962 to Verona, Italy, to receive the Prix d'Italia. (The same story, in a slightly altered form, appeared in *Talking to Myself* a couple years later.) It is a lighthearted tale of the ups and downs of a foreign traveler, particularly one who cannot speak the language of the country he is visiting. Called "Tipping Is an Art, Not a Science," it exemplifies the Studs Terkel who is always forgiven his excesses.[14]

In 1979 Terkel was one of 18 Chicagoans the *Tribune* invited to suggest to the newly elected mayor, Jane Byrne, what her priorities should be. He was in fact given top billing, complete with a photograph, befitting his place as Chicago's reigning pundit. He called her election victory, which pleased him, a big boost for the city and a cause for celebration. "We beat the bastards," he said, meaning the surviving but sputtering Daley machine. He said that the new mayor should build her grass-roots base by making people feel they belonged – both to a local community and to the larger city. She should above all preserve neighborhoods, halt the blind erection of condos and high rises, and return to the people a sense of power over their lives, particularly the most basic of human rights, to determine where and how they are going to live.[15]

Later that year, as Jimmy Carter was mired in the Iran hostage crisis and a Republican victory seemed likely the following November, Terkel helped found a new Citizens party. It was headed by Barry Commoner, who would be its presidential candidate, and it would try to appeal to nonvoters, the multitudes repelled by politics-as-usual.[16] This movement's populism and progressivism reminded Terkel of Fightin' Bob La Follette. Little came of the venture, as Illinois Representative John Anderson ran the next year as a liberal

Independent and took, in the popular vote, less than 8 percent to Carter's 42 percent and winner Ronald Reagan's 50 percent.

In 1980 Terkel's name reached the Supreme Court, at his own request. Earlier, under the new Freedom of Information Act, he had gained access to FBI files collected on him through the years, and now he demanded that he be allowed to see all files containing his name. He had been turned down in lower courts, and in January 1980 he was turned down by the highest court in the land. *Terkel v. Webster* went into the waste can.[17] Later in the year he was asked by the *Tribune* to name an issue important to the nation that was not being addressed by its leaders. He made no reference to the secrecy he had been fighting but said rather that most important was military spending. He called it obscene. East and West could now kill each other's citizens many times over, yet we were about to shell out another $10 billion for the MX missile system. It was sheer lunacy. That money could literally transform the American economy.[18]

The following year, in September 1981, he appeared before the congressional Commission on Wartime Relocation and Internment of Civilians. As always, he spoke for the underdog, in this case Japanese-Americans seeking reparations for having been imprisoned and stripped of jobs and property during World War II. Terkel proved to be an effective witness for the plaintiffs, despite not knowing much in the way of details. He had never before spoken out on behalf of Japanese-Americans. He had not even mourned for Hiroshima and Nagasaki when the atomic bombs fell. After doing "Born to Live" he felt differently. When asked by the commission how much money he thought would be appropriate to compensate the petitioners for their losses, he said honestly, "I think some dough should be involved. It can't just be an 'I'm sorry, dear.' "[19] There was laughter around the room, and tensions were relieved.

Awards continued to pile up. In 1981 Terkel received the Chicago Public Library's third annual Carl Sandburg Award for nonfiction, in recognition of his new book *American Dreams.*[20] At the end of the year the *Tribune* once again made him one of its celebrities, along with Ronald Reagan, Edward Kennedy, and Jerry Falwell, who were all asked, "How can peace on earth be achieved?" Terkel's answer was perhaps as predictable as that of the others in this motley crew. End the mad nuclear arms race, he said. The superpowers were nearing insanity in their game of "chicken," and they both should realize that in a world this dangerous no one could or should try to be number one. He quoted Albert Einstein's famous statement that while science has taken a quantum leap forward, man as a social being is still living in the Neanderthal Age.[21]

The Girard Affair

Working may today be Terkel's best-remembered and most-read book – and his most controversial. When it was published in 1974 a city librarian from Georgia wrote Terkel that someone had called to complain about the obscene book called *Working Studs* by Terkel. A different sort of protest was raised in 1982, this time against its content, particularly its language, and this time in Pennsylvania.

Early in 1982 Terkel received a telephone call from a high school teacher in Girard, a small city in northern Pennsylvania, near Lake Erie, telling him that she needed his help. She and *Working* were in some trouble. Terkel hopped on a plane, went to Girard, and challenged the teacher's challengers. What he did that February day demonstrates both his fierce dedication to freedom of speech and his cunning gift for self-promotion. It also says a great deal about Terkel's feel for the common man.

Girard is a working-class town of 2,500 people, most of them the kind Terkel has always felt he represented in his books. Karolyn Nichols, the high school teacher who called on him for help, had made *Working* a unit of her senior vocational English class several terms before and had never encountered organized resistance to it. She said she felt it gave her students splendid instruction in vernacular articulation and insight into the world of work they would soon be facing. Because she had never had opposition to it, she did not expect any from her 1982 class of 14 students. But that January, when she assigned passages that some of them and their parents considered "offensive," a number of her students, led by Robert Burns and Jim Richardson, folded their arms and refused to read the assignment. Nichols explained that it was required, but still they refused, labeling the book "profane." It seems that they took exception to the language of a speaker Terkel identified as a firefighter.

When Nichols refused first to drop the assignment and then to provide them, at their request, with alternative reading – considering their protest a rebellious infringement on her own freedom as an instructor – a parents' group was organized to fight her. Headed by Burns's mother, Linda, and a Baptist pastor, Lawrence Flatt, the group numbered at times as many as 30 members. The group told the Girard School Board that *Working* was profane and that it gave the kids a distorted, negative view of the work world. They said they had no desire to ban the book or to prevent those who wanted to read it from doing so, that all they asked was an alternative assignment for those who requested one. Five of the 14 students were by this time refusing to do the assignment.[22] It was at this point that Nichols put in her call to Terkel.

Terkel went to Girard at his own expense and spent 2 February visiting classes, particularly vocational English, accompanied by reporters. He later made some of his exchanges with students, mostly their comments to him, a part of his 1988 book *The Great Divide*. He left unedited their unsophisticated, often quaint, sometimes inarticulate, but still thoughtful, vital tone (*Great*, 47-50). During the session with vocational English the 17-year-old Jim Richardson, who said his ambition was to be a tool-and-die maker, challenged Terkel to read aloud the firefighter's testimony, the passage that was the source of their discomfort with and protest against the book. Terkel did so, although, significantly, he chose to substitute the word *dash* for each word the students considered profane. "What do you remember most – the words I dashed, or the thought he said?" Terkel asked them when he finished. "I leave it to you."[23] Whether they followed his logic is not known.

The implication of his remarks was that the message would have come through more clearly had the original words, profane or not, been retained. Terkel did not entertain the question of whether the message might have been made clearer by omitting the "words" altogether, and neither apparently did any of the students. Terkel had always said that he would not alter his speakers' words in this or any other way, except perhaps the order of paragraphs or the omission of whole sections, and so perhaps it never occurred to him that he had the right to remove the firefighter's profanity.

Toward the end of the hour Richardson admitted that he himself at times used such words, earthy Anglo-Saxonisms, but that even when he did he felt it was wrong. Reading it in a book, he said, made a word more socially acceptable, which led to its wider use. Thus

Working was socially destructive. He would not change his opinion about that, and he would not read the assignment. But at least one of the former resisters caved in to Terkel's logic, or perhaps to his charm, and changed his mind. "One or two bad words" should not condemn a whole book to oblivion, he reasoned, and he made a formal apology to Terkel for his previous behavior. Terkel was genuinely moved by what the boy said and concluded the class by saying, "Now I know why I came to Girard" (Robbins, 12).

Later that afternoon Terkel met in private session with the Girard School Board, and from their subsequent actions it seems that he won their support. Then at a parents' meeting that evening he ran into the proverbial hornet's nest. His own description of the session makes it sound chaotic, with one student popping up at regular intervals to shout Scripture verses while a mother accuses Terkel of the kinds of crimes the ancient Athenians cited in condemning Socrates to death. News accounts of the meeting agree. Jim Richardson's mother at one point cried, "You are corrupting the morals of our children," to which Terkel angrily replied, "I want to know what impels people to go through 700 pages to find so-called dirty words" ("Terkel," 5).

The whole business seemed to mystify Terkel. These were common people, his very own, and he was shocked to find them taking this attitude toward one of his books. "What astonishes, surprises, and disappoints me," he said, "is people picking up on something that's irrelevant" ("Terkel," 5). Perhaps irrelevant to Terkel, but not to everyone in Girard. He had run into a group of common people who did not think the way he thought all such people did. This vocal minority of Girard Terkel was unable to win over to his point of view. Members of the protest organization walked out before the meeting adjourned, their resolve hardened, now demanding not just an alternative reading assignment but that the book be banned from the vocational English classroom.

The Girard School Board announced that it would decide the fate of *Working* on 15 February, and the protest group announced that if they were not satisfied with its decision they would seek legal action. Jim Richardson's father, Robert, retained lawyer William Ball of Harrisburg to defend the three students who continued to hold out against reading the book should they be given no alternative to the requirement. High school principal Walter Blucas, on the other hand, announced that if the book were banned he would have to make a very serious professional decision. Meanwhile, the high school's junior class, perhaps sincerely, perhaps in part to show up the seniors who were protesting, sent Terkel a letter thanking him for coming to bring a bit of enlightenment to their school. On 9 February the parent protest group asked the school board to delay its decision so that emotions could subside and things get back to normal. The 15 February date was extended into March. During that cooling-off period Nichols offered the three holdouts an alternative assignment, but two of the three refused it, demanding still that the book be banned from their classroom.[24] Finally, on 22 March, acting on the recommendation of a subcommittee assigned the task of sorting through the various arguments, the school board voted unanimously not to ban the book. Not only was the banning of books against board policy, but the board said explicitly that it did not find *Working* inappropriate reading for high school seniors.[25] All 14 students would have to read the assignment, including the words of the firefighter, or receive a failing grade for that unit. "With all deference due the parents," the board concluded, "their sensibilities are not the full measure of what is proper education" (Schwarz, 1). Jim and Robert chose not to read the material and thus failed the unit.

Calling the board's decision "a triumph – for the teacher," Terkel said that any form of restriction on Nichols's freedom to assign whatever she deemed good for her students' education would have been censorship (Schwartz, 1). While he was pleased to see parents involved in their children's education, he was convinced that such moves to ban books would not occur if parents actually read the material they thought was offensive. Still, we are left with the nagging suspicion that Terkel preferred that the parental sensibilities match his own and that those with opinions contrary to his own keep quiet ("School," 2).

The Girard incident brought Terkel a great deal of national attention. Even before the school board's decision the *Nation* (in which, of course, Terkel owned stock) published an article calling on readers to stand with Terkel against this neo-McCarthyite effort at censorship.[26] After the decision was announced the *New York Times* commented that this and other recent moves to ban books from schools were born of frustration and fear. People who felt that they were losing control of their lives, those unable to protect their families and communities from overwhelming social and economic attacks they did not fully understand, were going for easy targets, hoping for a measure of revenge. They condemned dirty words, banned books, and censored teachers' lesson plans because they were impotent against their real enemies. Terkel was portrayed as a fighter for integrity and freedom of speech.[27]

Sales of *Working* and other Terkel oral histories still available in stores increased. His next book won a Pulitzer Prize. Controversy was profitable. *Chicago Tribune* columnist Bill Granger had predicted the windfall back in February when he groused, tongue-in-cheek, that he wished someone would ban one of his own books so that he could sell a few more of them, the way Terkel was bound to do.[28]

In May 1982 the *Washington Post* reported that Girard principal Blucas had told the two young holdouts that if they did not complete their *Working* assignment they would not pass their English course and would not graduate.[29] Karolyn Nichols has told me that this was never the case. Although Richardson and Burns did refuse to do the assignment and did fail the unit, this was one of several units during the term, and on average they had a passing grade. Both students graduated on time. There was never any question that they would not do so.

It is still not clear who won and who lost at Girard. Terkel certainly gained national stature as a champion of free speech. The school board successfully upheld the principle of academic freedom. The students learned some valuable lessons. The two holdouts, rebels with a cause, suffered for their convictions but not severely so, just enough to make them feel gallant. Nichols got more attention than most high school teachers do in a lifetime, rotated off the vocational English assignment, and watched as her successor chose not to continue using *Working* in the class. It was made abundantly clear that America's common man speaks with different voices, at least one of which Terkel prefers not to hear.

From the beginning of the controversy Terkel called the Girard people his own and vowed that above all he did not want to embarrass any of them.[30] He seems sincerely to have tried not to do so. While he was gratified to find that the overwhelming majority of people in Girard supported him – asking him to sign copies of his books, vowing their dedication to free speech – it was disturbing for him to learn that some commoners wanted to silence the speech of other commoners. All of which hints that the voices we find in the oral histories may be more carefully selected and edited than we know. It also hints at a form of mild elitism that Terkel would deny and perhaps not even recognize.

Politics

Girard only accelerated the pace of Terkel's rising fame and influence. In 1983 he took an active role in the Chicago mayoral election that ended in the victory of the first black man to sit in city hall, Harold Washington. In a speech endorsing Washington, Terkel said that in the 64 years he had lived in Chicago this was the first time he had felt he could vote for a mayoral candidate. It was the first time the city had known a credible candidate for the city's highest office. The town that had made itself proud by producing Louis Sullivan, Nelson Algren, and Richard Wright should now make itself even prouder by electing Washington. Terkel's support was hailed by the media as a sign of good race relations in a new era of Chicago politics.[31] Washington, elected with the support of white liberals, died in office, and Terkel lamented his untimely demise. At the next election, much to his chagrin, Chicago elected Richard J. Daley's son Richard M. Daley mayor. Just like his father, just another hack, Terkel calls him.

By 1984 Terkel's fame and celebrity had reached the point where he commanded between $5,000 and $10,000 for a public appearance, about the same, it was estimated by one newspaper, as that of advice columnist Ann Landers. For a time he did follow the lecture and speech circuit, but after a while he began cutting back. Now past 70 and already financially comfortable, he did not like being away from home, losing track of where he was, or gaining weight from too many fancy dinners and drinks with his fans. Money just was not that important to him.[32]

That year, 1984, which George Orwell had taught literate men to dread, Terkel was such a celebrity that when the *Chicago Tribune* did a story on hair care, of all things, he was asked to tell the newspaper how he managed his own. Obviously not considering this too frivolous a topic for a man of his influence, and choosing to make a philosophical-political statement along with providing entertainment, Terkel told the press that hair care is the mark of a man, that a man makes a philosophical and political statement when he decides where to go for such "care," what kind of professional to employ, and the style he will wear. As a populist, Terkel said, he was a barbershop man, for barbershops are designed for the common man. "I chemically couldn't go to a stylist," he said. He needed to smell the talcum and see the pole. He failed to explain why he let his hair fly loose, like some Old Testament prophet. When told that Chicago City Councilman Ed Vrdolyak used a stylist, Terkel said he was not in the least surprised. "Best commentary I've heard on him yet," he said.[33]

Despite celebrity and the trivialization it sometimes spawned, Terkel continued to live and speak his mind as he had always done. His lecture fee doubled after he won the Pulitzer Prize in 1985, but instead of taking advantage of the windfall to fill his bank account, he actually curtailed his appearances. Even when asked silly questions, he used the limelight fame brought him to explain with memorably pithy comments the principles of his form of liberalism. He did not soften his criticism of public figures who failed to do their duty to the common man.

Terkel's admiration for Fightin' Bob La Follette and his brand of progressivism never waned. In 1984 Terkel traveled to LaFollette's home in Madison, Wisconsin, to help celebrate the seventy-fifth birthday of La Follette's magazine, the *Progressive*. There he shared the stage with editor Erwin Knoll and Wisconsin Attorney General Bronson La Follette. When during his speech the sun suddenly popped out from behind a dark cloud, Terkel declared that it was proof that God was not with Ronald Reagan, despite his "come out into the sunshine" routine. It was saying, "I'm wit' ya, friends of fightin' Bob, I'm wit' ya."[34] It was an interesting comment coming from an avowed agnostic.

Terkel's admiration for La Follette, in part a childhood fixation, has made him contemptuous of most other politicians. One might think he would admire the "populist" Missourian Harry Truman, who has become something of a liberal icon, but he does not – partly because Truman, whatever his achievements, was the product of the Pendergast Machine, much like the Daley Machine of

Chicago, and partly because of Truman's decision to drop the atomic bomb on Hiroshima and Nagasaki. When La Follette's 1924 vice-presidential running mate, Burton Wheeler, told Terkel that 50 years earlier he had talked Truman out of abandoning politics when old Pendergast died, Terkel wondered if he had been wise to do so. When Wheeler allowed as how Truman had grown in the presidency, Terkel wondered if perhaps it only appeared that way, if indeed the rest of us had not merely shrunk (*Talking*, 12). Having carefully studied the decision to drop the atomic bomb on Japan, and having talked with its victims, Terkel was convinced that the bombing was an inhumane act, and a foolhardy one for the future of mankind. In his memoirs he contrasted Truman, "our tough little Give 'Em Hell President," with Albert Einstein, who was himself terrified of the bomb. "The way I figure it," Terkel muses, "if Einstein's scared, I'm scared" (*Talking*, 57).

As the years have passed, Terkel has spoken out ever more forcefully against the nuclear arms race and the political atmosphere that encourages it to continue. He might be expected to admire John Kennedy, considered by many a liberal president, but the way Kennedy handled nuclear power, threatening to use it so blithely, turned Terkel off. When *Washington Post* publisher Ben Bradlee came to WFMT to promote his book *Conversations with Kennedy*, Terkel planned to open the interview segment with the cello music of Pablo Casals, who had performed at the Kennedy White House, but Bradlee suggested that he play instead Kennedy's favorite song, "Big Bad John." Kennedy loved his tough-guy image. Had Khrushchev not turned his ships back from Cuba in 1962, Kennedy had told Bradlee and now Bradlee told Terkel, it would have meant World War III. "High Noon, by God," Terkel murmured in a state of shock (*Talking*, 57-60).

Terkel always saved his most savage attacks, however, for hizzoner Mayor Richard J. Daley. Terkel's memoirs virtually ooze with contempt for the man. He blamed Daley, whom he always referred to as the "Big Dumpling," for most of Chicago's ills: its institutionalized racism, its systematic destruction of historic buildings and traditional neighborhoods, its sellout to big business (*Talking*, 186). He once complained to Clifford Terry that if Father Andrew Greeley or "that WBBM clown John Madigan," both Daley supporters, were to write Chicago's official history, Daley would appear to be the greatest man since Jesus Christ. Daley-sycophant Greeley could always be counted on to appear, "picking canary feathers out of his teeth," after each and every Daley victory to sing his hymns of praise (*Talking*, 186-87). Daley's only talent, Terkel claimed, was for bookkeeping. He always knew exactly who owed him what, and he knew how to collect. His "success" story merely demonstrated that any hack could be elected mayor of Chicago six times (Terry, 9).

Terkel blamed Daley's bulldozers for wiping out whole neighborhoods in the name of progress and his cement mixers for erecting fortresses against which all attempts to build bridges of human brotherhood were wrecked. He told the German television crew that while even the pope is no longer considered infallible by his people, Richard Daley was nonetheless held to be incapable of error by too many Chicagoans (Siegert, 4). Terkel compared Richard Daley's Chicago to Pieter Botha's Johannesburg.

Terkel celebrated Daley's death in 1976 with an article that appeared in the *New York Times* but was not published in the Chicago papers. It was titled "For 21 Years, He Was the Boss, the Ultimate Clout," and in it he called the Daley tenure "surrealistic," the mayor himself a "totemic" figure, and his behavior while in office "Ozymandian." Daley was not really very astute politically. On the night he died, appropriately election night 1976, he had just lost the state of Illinois for his party's presidential nominee by hand-picking the wrong man to run on the ticket for governor. He was essentially just a ward heeler, good only at intelligence gathering, surveillance, and bookkeeping, at best a glorified watchman. His legacy was a segregated city, a school system that scandalized the nation, and neighborhoods ruined by urban renewal.[35]

Terkel welcomed the election in 1979 of Jane Byrne but soon lost his enthusiasm for her as well. She was a welcome change from Daley and his followers, but she was not change enough. He also welcomed the Harold Washington election and in this case did not lose his enthusiasm for Chicago's first black mayor. The year of Washington's election, 1983, Terkel wrote for the *New York Times* an analysis of the current political scene in his hometown, "The Chicago Machine Is a Junk Heap." The mayor is black, the council is independent, and the minorities are no longer field hands on the old Daley Plantation, he charged.[36] To this day Terkel keeps on the wall of his WFMT office a Pat Oliphant cartoon with the caption "Owing to the Death of Mayor Richard Daley, Chicago Trains Will No Longer Run on Time" (Terry, 7).

Terkel the social critic, professional gadfly, and political radical has always taken delight in making the "big guys" angry. He loves to espouse and advocate unpopular causes. Yet he survives, thrives, and adds to his fan club and influence with every passing year. Perhaps this is because he is so obviously sincere, honest, and consistent; perhaps it is because he has become such a celebrity that, right or wrong, he is bound to gain an ever-larger audience; and perhaps it is because he is so personally charming that even those who disagree with what he says and stands for admire the man. It certainly is not because he has the kind of friends who brandish guns on dark Chicago nights and say, "I will protect this guy."

A Star Is Born – at 65

For the past 15 years Terkel's celebrity status has been enhanced by his regular appearances on television and even in films, as well as by the appearances of his work on television and the stage. In 1975, when Bill Moyers was doing one of his periodic "to be or not to be" routines with his "Journal" and PBS needed a temporary replacement, its programming department decided to do a show called "Assignment America," to be hosted alternately by Studs Terkel, Doris Kearns, George Will, and Maya Angelou. Terkel opened with a piece on 36-year-old Ed Sadlowski, the young steelworker who had recently won a local labor election over the I. W. Abel candidate.[37] While Terkel and his co-hosts did a creditable job, the program had the look and feel of quick assemblage and a low budget, with just over $1 million allotted for 26 half-hour segments. After the first season the show was dropped when Moyers decided "to be" again.[38] Still, for a while Terkel went coast to coast for the first time since "Studs' Place" was canceled more than 20 years before.

From the start Terkel's books stirred creative imaginations. Because he was something of a playwright himself, his oral histories were arranged in dramatic sequences, almost as theater-in-the-round, and they almost asked to be staged. Nathaniel Benchley wanted to adapt *Division Street: America* for the stage but failed ever to come up with a workable scheme to produce it.[39] As noted earlier, Arthur Miller was so impressed *by Hard Times* that he used it as the basis for his play *The American Clock*, which opened in 1981. There were rumors that *Hard Times* would appear as a television miniseries, but plans for it failed to materialize. It was finally Terkel's third oral history, *Working*, that broke through to the stage.

Steven Schwartz was so impressed by *Working* when he read it in 1975 that he approached Terkel about adapting it for the stage – as a musical. Although Schwartz had been successful with the score he wrote for *Godspell* and had served as Leonard Bernstein's assistant in the production of *Mass*, Terkel was reluctant to grant his approval. Adapting oral history to the stage as a musical drama would be a departure from what Schwartz had done before, and Terkel had grave doubts it could be done. But Terkel finally agreed, Schwartz went to work, and in January 1978 *Working, the Musical* was ready to open. Sixteen actors played 40 Terkel characters, performing 15 musical numbers. It opened on 5 January at Chicago's Goodman Theater and ran for a month, then went on to Boston for another month, and finally, on 14 May, opened in New York (Cross, 15).

It was not a success. From the outset, critics complained that it was too long, a sure sign that it was boring, and that there were too many characters, too many ideas thrown out to the audience in too brief a time. Critics failed to find in it the sense of humor that characterized the book and concluded that the material's potential had not been realized. Terkel blamed Schwartz for the play's weaknesses, and their relationship deteriorated even as the production worked its way toward New York. By the time it opened at the Forty-sixth Street Theater Terkel was predicting that it would either be "a smash or a disaster,"[40] and he left it to fate, choosing not even to wait up for the morning editions to make their judgments. Terkel was in fact wrong, for the reviews were mixed (Peck, 22). The play was praised for its sensitivity and scorned for its shapelessness. It was not a bad play, but it was out of focus and needed tighter editing and perhaps a few better tunes (Terry, 7).

It hung on, precariously, "like a long-shot premature baby" Terkel said, and closed on 4 June. Terkel himself, during his brief visit to the city of his birth, stirred more interest and comment than did his play. D. B. Kaplain's Deli came out with a sandwich, the Studs Turkey, in his honor. For $4.50 one could have a breast of turkey garnished with tongue, Canadian bacon, shredded lettuce, and cranberry sauce served hot on French bread. While eating it one could take good old fashioned New York pride in a native son made good, even if that son preferred the barbarian Midwest to the cultured East (Terry, 6).

Even after the production closed in New York, *Working, the Musical* was far from dead. In 1981 it was taped for cable television with a stronger cast: Rita Moreno as a waitress, Eileen Brennan as a millworker, Charles Durning as a retiree, James Taylor as a truck driver, and Scatman Crothers as a garage attendant. Terkel himself introduced the production. Its 1981 premiere on Showtime was followed by a 1982 broadcast on PBS's "American Playhouse."[41] On the small screen the play was both a financial and a critical success. In 1985 *Working, the Musical* was brought back to the stage at Chicago's Different Drummer Music Theater with a modest set and simple format and received good reviews.[42] It seems likely to have periodic revivals.

By 1985 Terkel's books were considered good material for theater. That year *American Dreams*, adapted for the stage, made a brief but successful appearance at Chicago's Victory Gardens Theater. In 1988 *Talking to Myself* made its stage debut at Evanston's Northlight Theater. Northlight's artistic director, Russell Vandenbrucke, brought Paul Sills from New York to adapt and direct it. Seven actors, using Terkel's exact words, performed a series of scenes from the boyhood period of the book, the events from 1924 through 1936. It was well received locally but, like *American Dreams*, did not immediately go beyond Chicago.[43]

It was not just Terkel's oral histories that began to appear on stage and in films. The man himself, at an age when most men are preparing to retire, began a television and film career. When Harriette Arnow's novel *The Dollmaker* was adapted for the screen in 1984, Terkel was chosen to play a part in it. This story of Kentuckians heading for Detroit during World War II in hope of earning money enough to buy land back in the mountains starred Jane Fonda, Levon Helm, Geraldine Page – and Studs Terkel as a Detroit cab driver who took surreptitious nips from a bottle in a sack as he drove. As always, Terkel had to have a stand-in when the cab was in motion, "the only actor with one line who ever had to have one," he joked. He had more than one line, of course, and he did a more than credible job playing a jaded Yankee who had seen many Appalachian hearts broken. It is obvious from this cameo role that Terkel could have had as successful a career in film, playing character roles, as he had in radio.

In 1986 Terkel appeared in Ross Spears's documentary on the influence of the Civil War in American history, *Long Shadows*. Along with John Hope Franklin, C. Vann Woodward, Robert Penn Warren, Jimmy Carter, Robert Coles, and Tom Wicker, Terkel commented between and during scenes of contemporary southern life. He spoke specifically of the "nobility" and "romance" of the South. It lost the war, but it won the hearts of future generations. The North, he said, had no heroes like Robert E. Lee and Stonewall Jackson. He took the opportunity to remind viewers of all the "dough" the war brought to arms manufacturers, who became our first millionaire class.

In 1988, as he was busy finishing *The Great Divide*, Terkel took time to narrate a PBS documentary on the Abraham Lincoln Brigade in the Spanish Civil War. He also appeared in Gary Trudeau's HBO series about fictional presidential candidate Jack Tanner. As a last-ditch attempt to take the Democratic nomination from Dukakis, Tanner decides to name his cabinet before the convention opens. Along with Gloria Steinem for secretary of health and human services and Ralph Nader for attorney general, Tanner names Terkel secretary of labor. Terkel appears on camera, tongue firmly in cheek, to be interviewed about the honor. He says he will accept. "Everything's happening at once – and at my age," he says about the flurry of activity.[44]

He had just completed playing the part of Hugh Fullerton in the John Sayles film *Eight Men Out*, the story of the "Black Sox" scandal of the 1919 World Series. Based on a book by Eliot Asinof, the film recounts the way Fullerton uncovered the plot to throw the series and how his own Chicago paper refused to print the story. When it was printed, in the *New York Evening World*, it brought the scandal to light and led to the banning from baseball for life of eight players. "The thing I like about the film," Terkel said, "is that it attacks the sacred cows."[45]

Eight Men Out was filmed in Indianapolis and Cincinnati in order to have stadium and street scenes that were authentic. In both cities Terkel got his own dressing room, and he said that when he walked out onto the set he felt like Spencer Tracy. Unfortunately, when he saw the film he did not look much like Tracy. His best line, one he could well have written himself, came as the accused players were brought into court. A fellow reporter says that they are sure to be found guilty because of the evidence. Terkel as Hugh Fullerton replies, "This is Chicago, my friend. Anything can happen." It does. The guilty are acquitted, and it is the new baseball commissioner who bans the players. Terkel knows Chicago as Fullerton knew it: it has not changed much in 70 years.

One experience during the filming in Cincinnati gave Terkel a grand illustration for his persistent criticism of modern jargon. A journalist who was interviewing him suggested that they go to get "a bite." Terkel readily agreed, expecting to enjoy some good Cincinnati food – sausage, cabbage, beer. Instead they went to a television studio, and he learned that they were going for "a sound bite" for the evening news. "I'm still hungry," Terkel says (Auburn).

And So On

At age 80 Terkel continues to hold forth on WFMT, even though he says that working conditions there are uncomfortable for him under the new management, which cares for nothing but "the bottom line." He no longer smokes cigars, drinks in greater moderation, and has to wear a bothersome hearing aid. He plans to do as many more oral histories as time allows. One will be called "Enclaves," about unusual residential areas, and the other called "Rocking the Boat," about people who refuse to conform. But they will perhaps not satisfy his greatest dream: "I'd like to be at the foot of Calvary on that Friday with my tape recorder. The two thieves, those Roman guards, the disciples, the crowd, that subversive up there being executed by the government. I'd love to interview them all" (Auburn).

More than fame and wealth, Terkel once told Clifford Terry he wants "to have an impact on people, one way or another. To leave a mark, be remembered. That's a *big* ego-trip. The biggest in life" (Terry, 9). Terkel recalls that when Dorothy Day was asked why she got involved in social reform she said that she wanted to help create a world in which it would be easier for people to act decently: "That's me too," Terkel says with a twinkle (Auburn).

When asked about his own American dream, Terkel said it was to help secure food, clothing, shelter, education, and medical care for all, and even more to give people a sense of power over their own lives. "My goal is to survive the day," he explained. "To survive it with a semblance of grace, curiosity and a sense I've done something pretty good." On the other hand, he hastened to add, "I can't survive the day unless everyone else survives it too. I live in a community, and if the community isn't in good shape, neither am I" (Prescott, 120).

Notes and References

Preface

1. Benjamin DeMott, "Culture Watch," *Atlantic*, July 1977, 81; hereafter cited in text.
2. Herbert Mitgang, "Publishing: Prize Change," *New York Times*, 27 May 1977, sec. C, p. 23.
3. Norman Mark, "Studs Terkel: Division Street Philosopher," *Chicago Daily News*, 30-31 August 1969, 18; hereafter cited in text.
4. Tom Fitzpatrick, "The Hard Times of Studs Terkel," *Chicago Sun-Times*, 14 July 1970, 8; hereafter cited in text.
5. Joanne Koch, "Studs," *Chicago Tribune Magazine*, 6 December 1970, 84; hereafter cited in text.
6. Clifford Terry, "The Wide World of Studs Terkel," *Chicago Tribune Magazine*, 2 July 1978, 7; hereafter cited in text.
7. "A Caveat," in *Talking to Myself* (New York: Pantheon, 1977); hereafter cited in text as *Talking*.

Chapter One

1. *American Dreams: Lost and Found* (New York: Pantheon, 1980), xxiii; hereafter cited in text as *Dreams*.
2. *Chicago* (New York: Pantheon, 1986), 29; hereafter cited in text as *Chicago*.
3. Lee Michael Katz, "Pulling Truths from 'Real' People while Hiding Your Own," *Washington Post*, 6 February 1983, sec. B, p. 3; hereafter cited in text.
4. *Hard Times* (New York: Pantheon, 1970), 4-5; hereafter cited in texts as *Hard Times*.
5. "The Interviewer," *Newsweek*, 4 July 1976, 62-63.
6. Walter Oleksy, "My Most Unforgettable Christmas," *Chicago Tribune*, 25 December 1977, sec. 9, p. 6.
7. Ross Thomas, "Now You're Really Talking Terkel," *Washington Post*, 24 April 1977, sec. E, p. 1.
8. Steven Fiffer, "Fly, Bonnie, Fly!" *Chicago Tribune*, 7 November 1976, sec. 9, p. 55.

9. *Working* (New York: Pantheon, 1974), xvi; hereafter cited in text as *Working*.

10. "The Nelson Algren I Knew," *Chicago Tribune*, 13 May 1981, sec. 1, p. 16.

11. "His Foes Saw Red," *New York Times* (January 20, 1982), sec. A, p. 27.

12. Paul Galloway, "Probing the Private Life of the Public Studs Terkel," *Chicago Tribune*, 9 September 1984, sec. 3, pp. 1, 8; hereafter cited in text.

13. "Background on Studs Terkel," *Chicago Sun-Times*, 16 October 1984, 25.

14. "We Imagined an Eden," *New York Times*, 3 January 1971, sec. 2, p. 15.

15. Stewart McBride, "He's Called America's Greatest Oral Historian," *Christian Science Monitor*, 1 September 1983, sec. B, p. 4; hereafter cited in text.

16. "Image, Image on the Tube, Tell Me Who I Am," *Saturday Review*, 1 July 1972, 12-14.

Chapter Two

1. Rick Kogan, "Riding Home with Studs," *Chicago Tribune*, 29 November 1988, sec. 5, p. 2.

2. Eric Zorn, "Volume Turned up in WFMT Battle," *Chicago Tribune*, 15 August 1985, sec. 5, p. 13.

3. Conversation with James T. Baker.

4. *Giants of Jazz* (New York: Thomas Y. Crowell, 1957), 181-82; hereafter cited in text as *Giants*.

5. Program notes for the play *Amazing Grace*.

6. Ronald J. Grele, ed., *Envelopes of Sound* (Chicago: Precedent Publishing, 1975), 11; hereafter cited in text.

7. Raymond Schroth, "Between the Lines," *America*, 18 March 1967, 381; hereafter cited in text.

8. Peter S. Prescott, "The Great American Ear," *Newsweek*, 13 October 1980, 118; hereafter cited in text.

9. "On Understanding," *Nation*, 7 May 1973, 581.

10. "Letting Daylight into the Swamp," *Nation*, 20 April 1974, 501-2.

11. Geoffrey Wolff, "Talking to Americans," *Newsweek*, 20 April 1970, 116.

12. John Kenneth Galbraith, "Terkel's America," *Saturday Review*, September 1980, 64.

13. Address at Auburn University, 12 February 1990; hereafter cited in text as "Auburn."

14. Richard Walton, "Studs Terkel at Work," *Nation*, 4 June 1977, 696.

15. Nelson Algren, "Impressions of Studs as Bogus Frenchman and Urban Thoreau," *Chicago Tribune*, 14 September 1980, sec. 7, p. 5.

16. "Finding a Way out of Violence, Poverty, Racism, Corruption," *Today's Health*, December 1972, 38-44, 66-67, and "Is the Human Spirit Being Snuffed out in Our Cities?" *Today's Health*, January 1973, 43-47ff.

17. "Reflections on a Course in Ethics," *Harper's*, October 1973, 59-62, 67-72.

18. "Studs Terkel Talks with Arthur Miller," *Saturday Review*, 24 September 1980, 24.

19. "Jimmy Cagney and Studs Terkel," *Esquire*, October 1981, 106-8ff.

20. Nelson Algren, *Chicago: City on the Make* (Garden City, N.Y.: Doubleday, 1951), 30.

21. "Talk of the Town," *Newsweek*, 20 February 1967, 63; hereafter cited in text as "Talk of the Town."

22. *Division Street: America* (New York: Pantheon, 1967), xvii; hereafter cited in text as *Division*.

23. "Interviewing an Interviewer," *New York Times*, 19 August 1968, sec. C, p. 27.

24. Stewart Dybeck, "Terkel Shapes Its Voice Into a Charming Chorus," *Chicago Tribune*, 28 September 1986, sec. 14, p. 6.

25. Kathleen Madden, "Chicago with New Muscle," *Vogue*, March 1982, 361, 422-24.

26. William Brashler, "Touring America's Streets of Dreams with Studs Terkel," *Chicago Tribune*, 14 September 1980, sec. 7, p. 1.

27. Herbert Mitgang, "Books: Big Shoulders," *New York Times*, 16 October 1986, sec. C, p. 26.

28. Herbert Mitgang, "Publishing: The Talk of Chicago," *New York Times*, 13 June 1980, sec. C, p. 26; hereafter cited in text.

29. Peter Lyon, "Chicago Voices," *New York Times*, 5 February 1967, sec. 7, p. 3.

30. Michael Schlitz, review of *Division Street: America*, *Commonweal*, 7 April 1967, 101-2.

31. Richard Stern, "Farming the Tundra," *Nation*, 20 March 1967, 376-78.

32. Martin E. Marty, review of *Division Street: America*, *Book Week*, 15 January 1967, 1.

33. Andrew Greeley, "Wonderful Town," *Reporter*, 20 April 1967, 54.

34. Herbert Mitgang, "Squalls in the Windy City," *Saturday Review*, 28 January 1967, 36-37.

35. Judith Wax, "On the Move with Studs Terkel," *Chicago Tribune*, 30 March 1975, sec. 9, p. 20.

Chapter Three

1. See Terkel's conversation with the oral historians in Ronald J. Grele's *Envelopes of Sound*, as summarized in chapter 2 of this book.

2. Michael Frisch, *A Shared Authority* (Albany: State University of New York Press, 1990), 8; hereafter cited in text.

3. These guidelines are available from the Oral History Association, 1093 Broxton Avenue, Los Angeles, CA 90024.

4. See Anthony Seldan and Joanna Pappworth, *By Word of Mouth* (New York: Methuen, 1983), for a fuller account of such problems.

5. Christopher Lehmann-Haupt, "Transcripts of an Audiophile," *New York Times*, 13 April 1970, 39; hereafter cited in text.

6. Samuel Hand, "Some Words on Oral History," in *Oral History: An Interdisciplinary Anthology*, ed. David Dunaway and Willa Baum (Nashville, Tenn.: State and Local History Press, 1984), 53.

7. Gary Okihiro, "Oral History and the Writing of Ethnic History," in *Oral History*, ed. Dunaway and Baum, 197.

8. Richard Dorson, "The Oral Historian and the Folklorist," in *Oral History*, ed. Dunaway and Baum, 297.

9. "Hard Times Remembered," *American Heritage*, April 1970, 36-45.

10. "When Times Were Really Hard," *Atlantic*, April 1970, 73.

11. Henry Resnick, "When America Was Singing, 'Buddy, Can You Spare a Dime?' " *Saturday Review*, 18 April 1970, 27-30.

12. Richard Rhodes, "Hard Times," *New York Times*, 19 April 1970, sec. 7, p. 1.

13. L. E. Sissman, "Telling It the Way It Was," *New Yorker*, 16 May 1970, 152-54.

14. Nelson Algren, "Imaginary Pockets," *Nation*, 30 March 1970, 376.

15. Geoffrey Wolff, "Talking to Americans," *Newsweek*, 20 April 1970, 116.

16. Saul Maloff, "Life and Hard Times," *Commonweal*, 26 June 1970, 319.

17. Bernard Weisberger, review of *Hard Times*, *Washington Post Book World*, 19 April 1970, 4.

18. "Hard Times," *Times Literary Supplement*, 25 December 1970, 1510.

19. "Danger as a Career," *Harper's*, February 1974, 62-72.

20. "This Week's Arrivals," *Christian Century*, 10 April 1974, 402.

21. Peter S. Prescott, "Studs' Best Tapes," *Newsweek*, 1 April 1974, 76-78.

22. Bernard Weisberger, "Another Day Older and Deeper in Debt," *Washington Post Book World*, 5 May 1974, 1.

23. Charles Morrissey, "Making the System Go, Living with the Results," *America*, 27 April 1974, 331-32.

24. Editorial, *Chicago Tribune*, 28 April 1974, sec. 2, p. 4.

25. Benjamin DeMott, "Mules and Pinballs," *Atlantic*, August 1974, 76.

26. Susan Jacoby, "Not for Bread Alone," *Saturday Review*, 20 April 1974, 26-27.

27. Marshall Berman, "Everybody Who's Nobody and the Nobody Who's Everybody," *New York Times*, 24 March 1974, sec. 7, p. 1.

28. Thomas Smith, review of *Working, English Journal*, January 1976, 69.

29. Anatole Broyard, "Mr. Job on the Job: I," *New York Times*, 21 March 1974, 39.

30. Mary Daniels, "Working Folks Face Themselves on Stage," *Chicago Tribune*, 29 January 1978, sec. 6, p. 6.

31. Anatole Broyard, "Mr. Job on the Job: II," *New York Times*, 22 March 1974, 37.

32. Mike LaVelle, "Workers Speak for Themselves," *Chicago Tribune*, 6 January 1977, sec. 3, p. 4.

33. Abe Peck, "Studs Terkel's New Dreams," *Rolling Stone*, 13 July 1978, 8, 22; hereafter cited in text.

34. Christian Williams, "Studs Terkel: His New Project Is Power," *Washington Post*, 10 June 1974, sec. B, p. 1.

35. Robert Dahlin, "Studs Terkel's Latest Subject Is Himself," *Publishers Weekly*, 22 November 1976, 34.

36. Alden Whitman, "Studs Talking," *Chicago Tribune*, 10 April 1977, sec. 7, p. 1.

37. Robert Lekachman, "The Salt of Idiosyncrasy," *Saturday Review*, 30 April 1977, 18-20.

38. Nora Ephron, "A Higgledy-Piggledy Life," *New York Times*, 10 April 1977, Books section, p. 7.

39. John Leonard, "I Tape Therefore I Am," *New York Times*, 11 April 1977, sec. A, p. 25.

40. John Leonard, "Books of the Times," *New York Times*, 24 September 1980, sec. C, p. 29; hereafter cited in text.

41. Richard Christiansen, "*Talking* Offers Muted Views of Terkel's Life," *Chicago Tribune*, 8 September 1988, sec. 2, p. 9.

42. "Talking to Myself," *New Yorker*, 2 May 1977, 145-46.

Chapter Four

1. Alan Miller, "Books in Brief," *National Review*, 6 February 1981, 112.

2. Richard Kuczkowski, "National Town Meeting," *Commonweal*, 7 November 1980, 638.

3. Roderick Nordell, "The American Dream Revisited," *Christian Science Monitor*, 15 October 1980, sec. B, p. 3.

4. Robert Sherrill, "Looking at America," *New York Times Book Review*, 14 September 1980, 1.

5. Thomas Gannon, review of *American Dreams: Lost and Found*, *America*, 18 October 1980, 235.

6. Lawrence Goodwyn, "In the Right Kind of Trouble," *New Republic*, 15 November 1980, 32.

7. Barbara Grizzuti Harrison, "Is Joan Crawford Terrible?" *Nation*, 8 November 1980, 482-85.

8. Helen Epstein, "Tape It Again, Studs," *Washington Post Book World*, 5 October 1980, 4.

9. John Lahr, "Dreams of the Day," *Harper's*, January 1981, 72-76.

10. *"The Good War": An Oral History of World War II* (New York: Pantheon, 1984), note; hereafter cited in text as *"Good War."*

11. Paul Fussell, "The Real War, 1939-1945," *Atlantic*, August 1989, 32-48.

12. Garry Wills, "Terkel Brings the 'Good War' Home at Last," *Chicago Tribune*, 9 September 1984, sec. 14, p. 1.

13. William Goldstein, "Next Studs Terkel Book Recalls 'The Good War,' " *Publishers Weekly*, 6 July 1984, 39.

14. James Kaufmann, "Veterans Remember 'The Last Good War,' " *Christian Science Monitor*, 8 November 1984, 26.

15. Loudon Wainwright, "I Can Remember Every Hour," *New York Times*, 7 October 1984, Books section, p. 7.

16. Anatold Broyard, "Books of the Times," *New York Times*, 26 September 1984, sec. C, p. 20.

17. "Studs Terkel, Tribune's MacNelly Win Pulitzers," *Chicago Tribune*, 25 April 1985, 1.

18. "The Communicators," *Nation*, 11 May 1985, 548.

19. "Winners of Pulitzer Prizes," *New York Times*, 25 April 1985, sec. B, p. 10.

20. John Blades, "Prize-winner," *Chicago Tribune*, 26 April 1985, sec. 5, p. 1.

21. Mike Royko, "Vintage Whines from the Professors," *Chicago Tribune*, 20 May 1985, sec. 1, p. 3.

22. *The Great Divide* (New York: Pantheon, 1988), page following note; hereafter cited in text as *Great*.

23. Willie Morris, "Terkel's America," *Chicago Tribune*, 11 September 1988, sec. 14, p. 1.

24. Marilyn Gardiner, "Tape-recording the Crisis of the American Soul," *Christian Science Monitor*, 12 October 1988, 17.

25. Mel Elfin, "The Haves, the Have-Nots, and the Have-Somewhats," *New York Times*, 9 October 1988, sec. 7, p. 10.

26. Jacob Weisberg, "Soapstuds," *New Republic*, 28 November 1988, 38.

27. *Race: How Blacks and Whites Think and Feel about the American Obsession* (New York: The New Press, 1992); hereafter cited in text as *Race*.

28. *Publishers Weekly*, 3 February 1992, 70.

29. Douglas Foster, *Mother Jones*, May-June 1992, 3.

Chapter Five

1. Barbara Sherlock, "Terkel Says Center's for the Zombies," *Chicago Tribune*, 24 February 1984, sec. 7, p. 8.

2. Roderick Townley, "Let's Get Rid of All Those Know-It-All Pundits," *TV Guide*, 11 June 1988, 3-5.

3. "You Know Who I Seen?" *Nation*, 23 February 1974, 238-41.

4. James Wolcott, "Commoner than Thou," *Esquire*, February 1981, 17-18.

5. "Jurors Are Chosen to Select Winners of '73 Book Awards," *New York Times*, 12 November 1973, 25.

6. "Terkel Is Winner of Liebling Award," *New York Times*, 11 May 1975, 39.

7. "Ten Chicagoans Think Positively about the Future," *Chicago Tribune*, 5 January 1975, sec. 2, p. 2.

8. "Twelve Divergent Views of a Frenzied Year," *Chicago Tribune*, 28 December 1975, sec. 2, p. 1.

9. Linda Charlton, "The Senate Issue Is Not So Burning," *New York Times*, 13 April 1976, sec. A, p. 5.

10. "Support for the ACLU Is Urged," *Chicago Tribune*, 26 August 1977, sec. 1, p. 18.

11. "Ritt, Terkel Win Rights Award," *Chicago Tribune*, 13 December 1982, sec. 1, p. 14.

12. Deidre Carmody, "*Nation* Magazine Sold to Group Led by Hamilton Fish," *New York Times*, 23 December 1977, sec. A, p. 18.

13. Alice Siegert, "German TV Looks, but Fails to See," *Chicago Tribune*, 5 October 1977, sec. 4, p. 4; hereafter cited in text.

14. "Tipping Is an Art, Not a Science," *Vogue*, October 1977, 371.

15. "18 Chicagoans Suggest Top Priorities for Mayor Byrne," *Chicago Tribune*, 8 April 1979, sec. 2, p. 1.

16. Drummond Ayres, "Liberal Group Announces New Party," *New York Times*, 2 August 1979, sec. D, p. 17.

17. "F.B.I. Files," *New York Times*, 8 January 1980, sec. A, p. 17.

18. "Who'll Speak up on These Issues?" *Chicago Tribune*, 9 March 1980, sec. 2, p. 1.

19. Howard Tyner, "Witnesses Favor Payment to Japanese Internees," *Chicago Tribune*, 23 September 1981, sec. 1, p. 5.

20. "4 Receive Library Sandburg Award," *Chicago Tribune*, 26 October 1981, sec. 1, p. 12.

21. "Peace on Earth: Ideas to Reach an Elusive Goal," *Chicago Tribune*, 27 December 1981, sec. 2, p. 1.

22. William Robbins, "Terkel Defends Book after a Protest," *New York Times*, 3 February 1982, sec. A, p. 12; hereafter cited in text.

23. "Terkel Sticks to '*!X#," *Chicago Tribune*, 3 February 1982, sec. 1, p. 5; hereafter cited in text as "Terkel."

24. Donald M. Schwartz, "A Textbook Victory for Terkel's *Working*," *Chicago Sun-Times*, 23 March 1982, 1, 8; hereafter cited in text.

25. "School Board Backs Terkel's Book," *Chicago Tribune*, 23 March 1982, sec. 1, p. 2; hereafter cited in text as "School."

26. "Studs in Girard," *Nation*, 6 March 1982, 259-60.

27. Michiki Kakutani, "The Famed Will Gather to Read the Forbidden," *New York Times*, 5 April 1982, sec. C, p. 11.

28. Bill Granger, "Won't Somebody Please Ban My Books?" *Chicago Tribune*, 10 February 1982, sec. 3, p. 1.

29. "Reading Refusal Snags Pair," *Washington Post*, 23 May 1982, sec. A, p. 7.

30. Don Wycliff, "Studs Holds *Working* Session," *Chicago Sun-Times*, 3 February 1982, sec. 1, pp. 1, 8.

31. Vernon Jarrett, "2 More Voices in Mayoralty Sea," *Chicago Tribune*, 20 January 1983, sec. 1, p. 15.

32. Sam Smith, "Big Talkers," *Chicago Tribune*, 20 May 1984, sec. 10, p. 19.

33. Marlo Donato, "The Kindest Cuts," *Chicago Tribune*, 26 December 1984, sec. 7, p. 4.

34. Erwin Knoll, "Birthday Party," *Progressive*, November 1984, 4.

35. "For 21 Years, He Was the Boss, the Ultimate Clout," *New York Times*, 22 December 1976, sec. A, p. 29.

36. "The Chicago Machine Is a Junk Heap," *New York Times*, 17 April 1983, sec. 4, p. 19.

37. Les Brown, "Station Delays Terkel Program," *New York Times*, 11 January 1975, 59.

38. "TV: Channel 13's News Schedule," *New York Times*, 24 June 1975, 67.

39. Robert Cross, "Terkel Finally Gets Onstage," *Chicago Tribune*, 1 January 1978, sec. 9, p. 14; hereafter cited in text.

40. Linda Winer, "The 'City That Works' Takes Its Evidence to New York Stage," *Chicago Tribune*, 16 May 1978, sec. 2, p. 1.

41. John J. O'Connor, "TV: *Working* and Proposed Rights Amendment," *New York Times*, 13 April 1982, sec. C, p. 14.

42. Richard Christiansen, "Different Drummer Does Job in *Working*," *Chicago Tribune*, 10 October 1985, sec. 5, p. 7.

43. "Studs, the Play," *Chicago Tribune*, 6 September 1988, sec. 5, p. 3.

44. Herbert Mitgang, "Studs Terkel's Busy Year," *New York Times*, 22 September 1988, sec. C, p. 24.

45. "Dialing," *Chicago Sun-Times*, 10 August 1988, 43.

Selected Bibliography

PRIMARY WORKS

Books

American Dreams: Lost and Found. New York: Pantheon, 1980.

Chicago. New York: Pantheon, 1986.

Division Street: America. New York: Pantheon, 1967.

Giants of Jazz. New York: Thomas Y. Crowell, 1957, 1975.

"The Good War": An Oral History of World War II. New York: Pantheon, 1984.

The Great Divide: Second Thoughts on the American Dream. New York: Pantheon, 1988.

Hard Times: An Oral History of the Great Depression. New York: Pantheon, 1970.

Race: How Blacks and Whites Think and Feel about the American Obsession. New York: The New Press, 1992

Talking to Myself: A Memoir of My Times. New York: Pantheon, 1977.

Working: People Talk about What They Do All Day and How They Feel about What They Do. New York: Pantheon, 1974.

Articles

"All in a Day's Work." *Ms.*, June 1974, 64-68.

"American Dreams." *Washington Post*, 21 September 1980, sec. D, pp. 1, 5.

"Being a Woman in One of America's Most Scorned Families." *Today's Health*, February 1972, 48-53, 72.

"The Chicago Machine Is a Junk Heap." *New York Times*, 17 April 1983, sec. 4, p. 19.

"Danger as a Career." *Harper's*, February 1974, 62-72.

"Finding a Way Out of Violence, Poverty, Racism, Corruption." *Today's Health*, December 1972, 38-44, 66-67.

"For 21 Years He Was the Boss, the Ultimate Clout." *New York Times*, 22 December 1976, sec. A, p. 29.

"The Good War." *Atlantic*, July 1984, 45-75.

"The Good War." *Chicago Tribune*, 7, 8, 9, 10, 11 October 1984.

"Hard Times." *New York Times*, 20 December 1970, sec. 6, p. 10.

"Hard Times, 1970: An Oral History of the Recession." *New York Times Magazine*, 20 December 1970, 10-11, 46-51, 54.

"Hard Times Remembered." *American Heritage*, April 1970, 36-45.

"His Foes Saw Red." *New York Times*, 20 January 1982, sec. A, p. 27.

"Image, Image, on the Tube, Tell Me Who I Am." *Saturday Review*, 1 July 1972, 12-14.

"Is the Human Spirit Being Snuffed out in Our Cities?" *Today's Health*, January 1973, 43-47ff.

"James Cagney and Studs Terkel." *Esquire*, October 1981, 106-8ff.

"Letting Daylight into the Swamp." *Nation*, 20 April 1974, 501-2.

"The Nelson Algren I Knew." *Chicago Tribune*, 13 May 1981, sec. 1, p. 16.

"On Understanding." *Nation*, 7 May 1973, 581.

"Reflections on a Course in Ethics." *Harper's*, October 1973, 59-62, 67-72.

"Studs Terkel Talks with Arthur Miller." *Saturday Review*, 24 September 1980, 24ff.

"Tipping Is an Art, Not a Science." *Vogue*, October 1977, 351.

"We Imagined an Eden." *New York Times*, 3 January 1971, sec. 2, p. 15.

"When Times Were Really Hard." *Atlantic*, April 1970, 73-87.

"Women at Work." *Ramparts*, 4 April 1974, 38-44.

"You Know Who I Seen?" *Nation*, 23 February 1974, 238-41.

SECONDARY WORKS

Books

Algren, Nelson. *Chicago: City on the Make.* Garden City, N.Y.: Doubleday, 1951. Algren's impressionistic portrait of Chicago helped inspire and determine the style of Terkel's book *Chicago*.

Dunaway, David, and Willa Baum, eds. *Oral History: An Interdisciplinary Anthology.* Nashville, Tenn.: State and Local History Press, 1984. This collection of scholarly papers contains several chapters that shed light on Terkel as an oral historian: Richard Dorson's "The Oral Historian and the Folklorist," Samuel Hand's "Some Words on Oral History," and Gary Okihiro's "Oral History and the Writing of Ethnic History."

Frisch, Michael. *A Shared Authority.* Albany: State University of New York Press, 1990. Frisch's collection of articles on oral and "public" history helps place Terkel into the broader context of his field. The critical review of *Hard Times* is particularly enlightening.

Grele, Ronald J., ed. *Envelopes of Sound.* Chicago: Precedent Publishing, 1975. This record of an oral history conference contains pertinent remarks by Terkel and others about his and their methods of doing oral history.

Seldon, Anthony, and Joanna Pappworth. *By Word of Mouth.* New York: Methuen, 1983. This is an excellent examination of the pitfalls and rewards of doing oral history. It provides guidelines for evaluating the work of Terkel and others in the field.

Articles

Algren, Nelson. "Imaginary Pockets." *Nation*, 30 March 1970, 376-78. A portrait of Terkel by one of his best friends.

Blades, John. "Prize-winner." *Chicago Tribune*, 26 April 1985, sec. 5, p. 1. Critics question whether Terkel deserves the Pulitzer Prize and the title oral historian.

Brashler, William. "Touring America's Streets of Dreams with Studs Terkel." *Chicago Tribune*, 14 September 1980, sec. 7, pp. 1, 5. A review of *American Dreams.*

Broyard, Anatole. "Books of the Times." *New York Times*, 26 September 1984, sec. C, p. 20. A review of *"The Good War."*

———. "Mr. Job on the Job: I." *New York Times*, 21 March 1974, 39. "Mr. Job on the Job: II." *New York Times*, 22 March 1974, 37. A two-part review highly critical of *Working.*

Cross, Robert. "Terkel Finally Gets Onstage." *Chicago Tribune*, 1 January 1978, sec. 9, pp. 14-18. A story on *Working, the Musical*, based on Terkel's book *Working.*

Daniels, Mary. " 'Working' Folks Face Themselves on Stage." *Chicago Tribune*, 29 January 1978, sec. 6, p. 6. Witnesses from *Working* see the stage version of their book.

DeMott, Benjamin. "Culture Watch." *Atlantic*, July 1977, 81-85. A portrait of Terkel on the publication of *Talking to Myself.*

Fitzpatrick, Tom. "The Hard Times of Studs Terkel." *Chicago Sun-Times*, 14 July 1970, 8. Terkel during the Great Depression.

Galloway, Paul. "Probing the Private Life of the Public Studs Terkel." *Chicago Tribune*, 9 September 1984, sec. 3, pp. 1, 8. An attempt to reveal some of Terkel's carefully concealed private life.

Greeley, Andrew. "Wonderful Town." *Reporter*, 20 April 1967, 53-54. A review of *Division Street.*

Lehmann-Haupt, Christopher. "Transcripts of an Audiophile." *New York Times*, 13 April 1970, 39. A review of *Hard Times.*

Katz, Lee Michael. "Pulling Truths from 'Real' People while Hiding Your Own." *Washington Post*, 6 February 1983, sec. B, p. 3. A study of Terkel's passion for privacy.

Knoll, Erwin, "Birthday Party." *Progressive*, November 1984, 4. Terkel attends a meeting of La Follette admirers.

Koch, Joanne. "Studs." *Chicago Tribune Magazine*, 6 December 1970, 84-86. A portrait of Terkel at the publication of *Hard Times*.

Leonard, John. "I Tape, Therefore I Am." *New York Times*, 11 April 1977, sec. A, p. 25. A review of *Talking to Myself*.

McBride, Stewart. "He's Called America's Greatest Oral Historian." *Christian Science Monitor*, 1 September 1983, sec. B, p. 1. A discussion of Terkel's methods in looking for America's voice.

Madden, Kathleen. "Chicago with New Muscle." *Vogue*, March 1982, 361, 422-24. Terkel answers questions about his hometown.

Mitgang, Herbert. "Studs Terkel's Busy Year." *New York Times*, 22 September 1988, sec. C, p. 24. All about the way Terkel's career was exploding that year.

Peck, Abe. "Studs Terkel's New Dreams." *Rolling Stone*, 13 July 1978, 8, 22. A review of *Working, the Musical*.

Royko, Mike. "Vintage Whines from the Professors." *Chicago Tribune*, 20 May 1985, sec. 1, p. 3. Royko answers critics who doubt that Terkel deserved to win the Pulitzer Prize.

"Studs in Girard." *Nation*, 6 March 1982, 259-60. A comment on the controversy over *Working*.

Terry, Clifford. "The Wide World of Studs Terkel." *Chicago Tribune Magazine*, 2 July 1978, 6-7. A portrait of Terkel midway through his oral histories.

Townley, Roderick. "Let's Get Rid of Those Know-It-All Pundits." *TV Guide*, 11 June 1988, 2-5. Terkel comments on television coverage of political campaigns in an election year.

West, Hollie. "Talking Terkel." *Washington Post*, 27 November 1980, sec. C. p. 1. A portrait of Terkel on the publication of *American Dreams*.

Winer, Linda. "The 'City That Works' Takes Its Evidence to New York Stage." *Chicago Tribune*, 16 May 1978, sec. 2, p. 1. A story on *Working, the Musical*.

Wolcott, James. "Commoner than Thou." *Esquire*, February 1981, 17-18. A portrait of Terkel as champion of the common man.

Wycliff, Don. "Studs Holds *Working* Session." *Chicago Sun-Times*, 3 February 1982, 1, 8. Coverage of the controversy over *Working*.

Index

The Author

James T. Baker earned his Ph.D. at Florida State University in 1968 and since then has taught history and directed the university honors program at Western Kentucky University. He has published more than 100 articles and nine books, including studies of Catholic poet Thomas Merton, philosopher-longshoreman Eric Hoffer, novelist and social critic Ayn Rand, Congressman Brooks Hays, and President Jimmy Carter. He has twice been a Fulbright Senior lecturer (in Korea in 1977 and in Taiwan in 1984) and has directed six programs in England and Scotland under the auspices of Kentucky's Cooperative Center for Study in Britain. In 1988 and 1990 he conducted the center's term at Oxford.